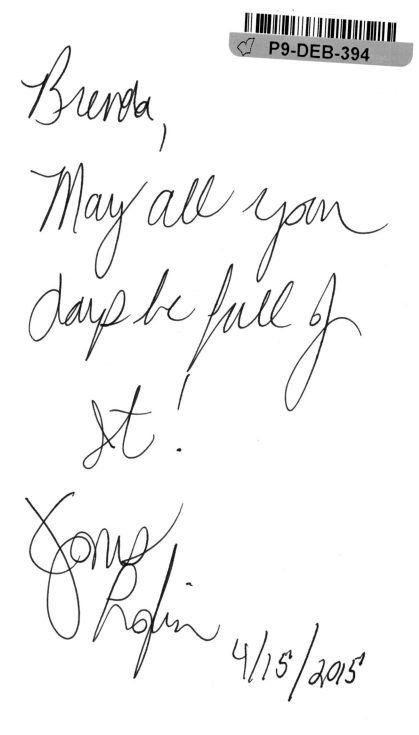

Brenda,

May all your

days be full of

it!

Sonya

Rofin

4/15/2015

Getting to It

ALSO BY JONES LOFLIN AND TODD MUSIG

Juggling Elephants

Getting to It

Accomplishing the Important,

Handling the Urgent,

and Removing the Unnecessary

Jones Loflin
and
Todd Musig

HARPER
BUSINESS

An Imprint of HarperCollins*Publishers*
www.harpercollins.com

HarperCollins books may be purchased for educational, business, or sales promotional use. For information, please e-mail the Special Markets Department at SPsales@harpercollins.com.

FIRST EDITION

Designed by Fritz Metsch

Library of Congress Cataloging-in-Publication Data has been applied for.

ISBN 978-0-06-228242-2

13 14 15 16 17   OV/RRD   10 9 8 7 6 5 4 3 2 1

To our families,

who are always the IT for us

Acknowledgments

There were many times during the past four years when we wondered if *Getting to It* would ever get done. We found ourselves constantly reaching into the manuscript itself for guidance and the motivation to stay focused on the writing and editing of the message. This finished book, however, would never have been completed without the help of some incredible people with whom we shared the journey and to whom we are eternally grateful.

It was Dr. Spencer Johnson who gave us the initial motivation and direction after we had the idea for *Getting to It*. We will forever remember his excitement, encouragement, and sage advice over dinner in San Diego several years ago. He has always taught us to "keep it simple because simple solutions can surprisingly be the most powerful," and we have tried to follow his words with this book.

To say we have the best literary agent in the world is not a fair statement. We have the best coach, cheerleader, reviewer, constructive critic, *and* literary agent in Margret McBride. She never ceases to surprise us with her insight and ability to look at the big picture of writing and publishing books. Her assistant, Faye Atchison, is no less amazing. Faye's attention to detail with proposals and contracts helped all of us keep our sanity. And her personable nature makes her a delight to work with.

We are extremely excited to be a part of the HarperBusiness imprint. It became clear to us very quickly that Hollis Heimbouch and Colleen Lawrie got "It." From support of this project to jacket design to editing and marketing, we are thankful for their vision of what this book can mean to so many people.

For the message of any book to be received well, it must be written well. Dennis Mathis of Close Readers was invaluable in the initial edits of the manuscript, making the flow more natural, the words more descriptive, and the concepts more clear.

From our early days of talking with Dr. Johnson we have known that feedback, while painful, is essential to creating a superior book. We are so appreciative of friends, family, and clients who read different versions of our manuscript and took the time to provide input that made the book stronger and of greater value.

Finally, we cannot end these acknowledgments without saying thanks to two other groups of people. We can never repay our wives, Lisa and Wendy, for putting up with our wild ideas and being patient as we spent time away from each of them to make this book a reality. And to our children—Alex, Sydney, Vashti, Tayva, and Jacquelyn—it is you who gave us the daily validation that time is too precious to be focused on anything other than that which is most important.

Contents

Getting to It

Chapter 1

What Is It?

IN YOUR STRUGGLE TO GET IT *ALL* DONE, WHAT'S
NOT GETTING DONE?

At any time of day, do you find yourself saying "When
I get time, I will . . ." or "One day when things are different . . ." and then realizing how familiar that sounds?
Do you reflect on the past five years and become frustrated because you've yet to accomplish all the things
you promised yourself you'd get to by now?

What if a high percentage of your tasks and actions were actually contributing toward accomplishing
those things that matter to you? What if you felt as if
you actually had time to help other people, giving full
attention to the needs of coworkers and customers?

What about life outside of work? What if you actually enjoyed taking your children to their activities and
got your errands done in a quarter of the time it takes

you now? What if some of the chores on your list became more enjoyable because you're confident in your ability to get your most Important Things done?

Would you laugh more often and feel more at ease? Would you feel respected and appreciated by clients, friends, neighbors—and even, wonder of wonders, by your teenage children?

Would that be enough of a reason for you to continue reading this book?

What if your schedule allowed more time for personal growth, and you could finally give a higher priority to relaxing and enjoying life? What benefits might result from having the time and enthusiasm to pursue the passions that energize you, inviting you to tackle the long-postponed "if only" items on the bucket list of things you'd like to experience in your life?

It's not that you haven't tried to become more organized and efficient many times in the past. You might even use a daily planner or manage your to-do list electronically. You may have a smartphone with buttons worn away from your furious attempts to answer all of your e-mail on the go.

It's possible that other people already admire you as someone who has it all together. Do you privately wonder how much longer you can maintain your pace and your reputation for always delivering on time? Are you often merely getting by rather than thriving, hoping that something (other than retirement or winning the lottery) will come along to rescue you from this stormy ocean of hurry, deadlines, and the constant juggling act of balancing never-ending work and life demands?

What Is It?

There is a solution to help get you focused and pointed in the right direction. In a word: IT. Define IT. Plan IT. Focus on IT. Get others excited about IT. Celebrate IT. And then plan for the next IT. Consider this definition:

MAIN ENTRY: It

PRONUNCIATION: \'it\

FUNCTION: Noun/pronoun followed by action

DATE: Today

DEFINITION: The most Important Thing

IT will save you from the avalanche of possibilities that await you every day at work. IT will make the difference in your reaching your full potential and your desired level of success. IT will help you develop and appreciate supportive, positive relationships. IT will guide you in defining who you are as an individual and as a professional, and in clarifying what is important to you.

"That's it?" you say.

Yes, that's IT. It's that simple.

Asking yourself, Of all the paths I could take, which

is the most important at this moment? may at first seem simplistic and obvious, and no different from what you do now.

The problem, you tell yourself, isn't in deciding what must be done; often circumstances or other people have made those decisions for you. The problem is in all the steps required to actually accomplish a number one priority.

For example, a marketing director might identify IT as a badly needed strategy for launching the company's new product. That part was easy. Execution is something quite different. Finding the time to devote to IT, getting people who are currently overloaded and already moving in twenty different directions to focus on IT, and securing the necessary financial resources from an already strained budget are far from simple tasks. The very next step after IT has been defined can result in frustration and delay. Maybe, in this example, the marketing director senses that a sales incentive strategy—a whole new, complex IT—has to be developed to support the new marketing strategy. How does he decide which is the priority?

As you will see in the chapters to come, identifying IT isn't just the first step in a process, it's *every* step.

Constantly stepping back and analyzing what's driving your choice of IT is more than just a useful exercise, it's critical. Clarity of thought and purpose is necessary not only in determining IT, it's essential to

IT: of everything you could do in the next moment, the most IMPORTANT THING.

efficiently organizing all the steps required to accomplish IT.

Certainly, defining one IT at the outset is crucial. Getting IT wrong can have disastrous consequences for individuals as well as entire organizations. Also, leaving IT undefined can cause priorities to be at cross-purposes with one another, making your days busy but rarely productive or meaningful.

Consider a few examples:

- The week you had a deadline approaching for a report, you chose to work on less important tasks because you weren't thrilled about working on IT.
- Upon walking into your office in the morning, you turn on your computer and open up your e-mail. Nine hours later, you have spent the entire day basically managing your e-mail as it comes into your box. Nothing of significance has been accomplished.
- Your child is riding her bike without training wheels for the first time. When she calls, "Look at me!" you call back, "I see you." But the fact is, your preoccupation with office work had your mind a thousand miles away, and you hadn't actually seen her first wobbly minutes as a bike rider.
- Taking an hour for yourself to engage in your favorite hobby or just relax creates guilt and anxiety, because you constantly feel as if there's something more important you should be doing.

So where do you begin? How do you ensure that you know what IT is and that you have the opportunity to work on IT today?

Types of Its, and the Need to Identify Them

At the risk of sounding like Dr. Seuss: There are big ITS and little ITS, easy ITS and difficult ITS. There are ITS that make you want to get out of bed in the morning and ITS that make you want to hide under the bedcovers all day.

ITS can be classified according to their time scales. Long-term ITS might range from your lifetime achievements (becoming a successful parent, a loving spouse, a pillar of the community, a world-class musician) to goals that require only a year or two to accomplish. For organizations, a long-term IT could take five or more years to complete.

Short-term ITS are goals you want to accomplish in six months to a year. You may find that this type of goal setting is the most typical kind in your life—losing weight, overcoming that hitch in your golf swing, repainting the house, learning Italian. Since childhood, you've learned the importance of working day by day toward such goals: you can't become fluent in Italian the night before your flight to Rome. For organizations and entrepreneurs, short-term ITS—implementing a new software system, relocating manufacturing to a

new building, or securing funding—may take one to
three years to accomplish.

Daily ITS are the "here and nows." Most often,
they're in competition with a thousand other demands
on your time and energy. Over the course of a day, you
may encounter numerous paths that could be taken,
but probably only two or three really lead to completing today's IT.

It's important to define IT frequently as you move
through your day. Routinely defining IT creates an
opportunity to ensure you are on the right path, prepared to accomplish the most critical task of each moment. Consider these examples:

- Look at successful athletes. They never stop
  focusing on doing their best, whether in competition
  or during practice.
- Think about productive coworkers around you.
  Factoring out lunch, breaks, and interruptions, they
  rarely focus on something other than their work.
- Watch any true artist (painter, dancer, singer,
  musician, etc.) display his or her skill. When
  performing, they don't allow any thoughts to enter
  their minds that are not related to creating a stellar
  performance.

Such people spend an enormous amount of their
time and mental focus thinking, planning, and evalu-

ating every motion toward one purpose: the successful accomplishment of their overriding task or goal.

When you identify your IT for any period of time, you start a process of planning to make IT successful. Just asking, What is my IT in the next minute? sharpens your focus and helps ensure the right things get done in those sixty seconds.

The longer the period of time needed to accomplish IT, the more detailed the process and strategies might need to be to ensure that IT gets done. As we mentioned earlier, ITS come in all sizes.

Let's examine the need to focus on IT with a situation that might occur in the typical workday of Sam, a manager at a large insurance company. His IT for the next sixty minutes is to craft a job description for a new position within his department. He begins with the best intentions, reviewing his notes and data from the past six months. Three minutes into this demanding mental task, he hears the ding of an e-mail notification and glances up to see whom it's from. He doesn't read the message, but it's now on his mind, and he keeps wondering if he should check it out. He chooses to return to his primary task, but the mere act of thinking about e-mail has gotten him off track. He rereads what he's written, picks up his train of thought, and adds a couple of sentences. Then his phone rings. He doesn't answer it, but he looks to see who it is. It's Belinda. His mind races as he wonders what it is that Belinda might want. He resists the urge to answer the call because he knows he needs to get this job description done!

Sam is now thirty minutes into his IT. Some superb ideas are taking shape . . . just as Julie approaches him about a vacation-scheduling issue. Sam would like to put Julie off, but he knows he's been avoiding her about this for a few days. Sam tells her he has only twenty minutes before his next meeting, but he'll try to help her. After a brief review of the department's vacation schedule, Sam grabs his materials and leaves for the meeting.

At the end of the day, when Sam reflects on the fact that he never completed drafting the job description, he may rationalize that he had too many interruptions, too many real-world priorities that couldn't be ignored. Is that true, or could he have made different choices and focused on his goal?

Was his office the best place to work on IT? Was there a different place where Sam could have avoided the interruptions of nearby coworkers, a ringing phone, or e-mail notifications? What if he had closed his e-mail program before he started IT? And what about the coworker whose own priority was the vacation-scheduling issue? Could he have delegated this issue to her, asking her to talk to the two people with a conflict and see if they could find their own compromise? And the ringing phone—could he have established with his associates a reputation for responding quickly to voice mail, but on his own schedule? The bottom line is, there probably was much Sam could have done to accomplish his IT of drafting a job description if he were more consistent about staying focused.

Two Reasons for Your Struggle

Before we get too far along with the concept of IT, let's take a step back and look at two possible root causes of the average person's struggle to stay focused and productive. Each will be fleshed out more in the chapters that follow.

To better understand the first basic cause, picture in your mind a funnel that you take with you everywhere you go. Your funnel is determined by your education, experiences, and environment—representing all possibilities that exist for you. This funnel helps you capture all of the things you could do or become. Poured into this funnel are a variety of opportunities, tasks, dreams, big ideas, and plans. Your daily interactions and activities affect what goes into it: what your parents expected of you; your plans when you finished high school or college; the thoughts you have about starting a new business, working in a large organization, volunteering for causes, doing something creative, building your own home, or selling everything and moving to New Zealand to raise sheep—all flow into your funnel.

Because a funnel narrows at the bottom, all of these possibilities vie to become IT. But without a structure or process to manage them, you struggle to determine what is important, urgent, or unnecessary. "That's my world," you could say. "Every day is full of a million things I could do."

You're right. In fact, your funnel may be so full that it often overflows. Some possibilities may get pushed to one side because of interruptions, delays, relationships, or changes—and never make it through the funnel. The key to resolving this struggle then becomes determining the answers to these questions: What am I putting into my funnel? and What is actually coming out of my funnel and getting done?

A failure to audit what is getting into the funnel and not strategically focusing on what actually is coming out (getting accomplished) can cause disastrous results. Consider the budding entrepreneur and wannabe successful small-business owner. The list of all the activities that are required to start up or keep the business going can be endless. Activities like getting a business license; finding a location; buying a computer system; learning to use that system once you buy it; setting up an Internet connection; building a Web site; selecting health insurance and liability insurance; doing payroll, state taxes, federal taxes; designing and printing business cards; getting a post office box and a postage machine; buying packing materials, office supplies, office furniture, office equipment (fax, photocopier, a server, a phone system); opening a bank account; putting money in the bank account, hiring help, keeping the help happy, and don't forget the all-important taking out the garbage. As you can imagine, there are a lot of tasks being dumped into that funnel. Oh, and in the meantime, you need to come up with a product, manufacture the product, and, most important, find customers who will actually pay you money for the product. It's so easy to get caught in all the "stuff" that it takes to start and run a business that a lot of entrepreneurs fail because they don't focus on the key items, like finding paying customers.

As the owner of your life, you can fall into the same trap:

- "You are so busy making a living that you forget to have a life" (Dolly Parton).
- You get caught up in the "thick of thin things" and forget about what truly is important.
- You focus so much on the process or means to the end of doing things that you overlook the question, Why am I doing this?

Not having a plan also contributes to your failing to get your priorities accomplished. If you don't create a plan (and follow through with it) to tackle your priorities, something else will flow in to fill the void. We call this the Law of the Vacant Lot: if you don't plan for and act on how you will use a vacant lot, nature or squatters will move in and make those decisions for you. Weeds grow, trash accumulates, and unwanted creatures may even begin to make your vacant real estate their home.

The same principle applies with respect to how you use your time. If you don't determine the most important use of your time and act accordingly, something less desirable will consume it.

You can see this law in action in the way some people use e-mail. They say, "When the e-mail system goes down, everything stops. There's nothing we can do." But ask yourself, if that were true, how did anything—including the Hoover Dam, the interstate highway system, the eradication of smallpox—get accomplished before the invention of e-mail? While there are some organizations, positions, or situations that absolutely depend on e-mail communications, in most cases people have simply allowed e-mail to usurp a large part of their day and have allowed it to become their business's sole source of communication. The end result is that a few urgent items get done and lots of unnecessary tasks are undertaken, but not enough genuinely important tasks get accomplished.

In the training program we based on our book *Juggling Elephants*, participants are asked to identify their poor time-management habits. One participant said, "Social media." He explained, "I spent two hours on

*If you don't plan for and
act on how you will use
a vacant lot, nature or
squatters will move in and
make those decisions
for you.*

social media the other night when I really didn't mean to." He said he had intended to log on for only about ten minutes, but the time simply got away from him.

Without a well-conceived plan for how you're going to spend your time, almost anything can arise to distract you from what you really want to accomplish.

The Law of the Vacant Lot also can remind you that failing to choose IT right now has additional consequences: the task grows more difficult when it's necessary to backtrack from an unwise decision, remove obstacles that have materialized, and then proceed to make your desired outcome a reality. Saying things such as "When I'm older . . ." "When the children grow up . . ." "When I have more energy . . ." or "When my job is less stressful . . ." might only make pursuing IT more difficult whenever "when" finally arrives. Needing first to get older, younger, thinner, smarter, or richer . . . there are plenty of excuses for not getting started on IT. Every moment spent waiting to work on IT might result in something you never intended taking root on your vacant lot.

Napoleon Hill, the author of *Think and Grow Rich* and one of the pioneer philosophers in the field of personal success, gave some wonderful advice when he wrote, "Do not wait; the time will never be 'just right.' Start where you stand, and work with whatever tools you may have at your command, and better tools will be found as you go along."

It's Time to Get to Work on It

Is the value of IT becoming clear? Think of the difference it would make if you identified the most important of the possibilities facing you in every moment of every day—and worked to accomplish IT. Okay. "Every moment" may seem a little unrealistic, but what if you were able to increase your focus on the important by 20 to 30 percent? Wouldn't that make a difference in what you accomplish?

As Sam Nunn, the former US senator from Georgia, wrote, "You have to pay the price. You will find that everything in life exacts a price, and you will have to decide whether the price is worth the prize." The question for you is: What price are you paying for allowing things of lesser importance to dominate your schedule instead of spending more time on those you care most about?

Michelangelo, the Italian Renaissance painter, sculptor, architect, poet, and engineer, is famous for his fresco painting on the ceiling of the Vatican's Sistine Chapel and for his sculptures the *David* and the *Pieta*. Centuries after his death, his works still express his exceptional power, persistence, and passion. Few of us can imagine the level of intensity of purpose it takes to chisel an entire sculpture from a huge block of marble. Michelangelo clearly knew the value of IT.

He wrote about his work process, "I saw the angel

What price are you paying for allowing things of lesser importance to dominate your schedule instead of spending more time on those you care most about?

in the marble and carved until I set him free. . . . The sculptor's hand can only break the spell to free the figures slumbering in the stone."

Are you ready to break the spell that's been keeping you from IT? Prepared to create the productive workdays, strong relationships, or personal achievements that are stuck within you? Grab your chisel, and let's get to work on accomplishing the important, handling the urgent, and cutting away everything that's not IT.

Chapter 2

Defining It

DEFINE **IT,** OR EVERYTHING ELSE WILL
DEFINE YOU.

What does your current plan for getting your most Important Things accomplished look like? A long list of to-dos that creates another type of chaos as you seek to insert them into an already overcrowded schedule? How have you determined what gets done and what doesn't?

As discussed in chapter 1, What Is It?, an IT can range from a lifetime goal to an item that needs to be accomplished in the next thirty seconds, so the amount of time required to define IT varies with each situation. Determining where you want to go for dinner shouldn't take as long as deciding a company's next product or service. How do you handle that "IT of the moment"? How do you narrow the list and define what IT is for you? The process we suggest consists of five steps:

1. Stop what you're doing for a moment.
2. Review your funnel.
3. Evaluate your possibilities.
4. Use your filters.
5. Develop plans to say no to everything that's not IT.

Stopping for a Moment

Begin by stepping back. A key challenge for people with too much to do is that they are overwhelmed with so many potential activities that they don't know where to start or how to determine what should or shouldn't get done. The typical solution is just to tackle the task that is most convenient or enjoyable and work as long and as fast as possible, or focus on the task that is screaming the loudest for attention. This approach would be like bailing water from a leaking boat without figuring out how to fix the hole.

While working on IT is often hard, not working on IT can be even more exhausting in the long run, and, as you already may have discovered, it's ultimately futile in actually getting to what is most important.

This also is the time to reflect on why so many possible paths exist for you. In other words, it's time to review the opportunities in your funnel.

Let your first IT be to stop.

Reviewing Your Funnel

We discussed in chapter 1, What Is It?, how our mental funnel does the initial work of helping us determine what gets done. Possibilities enter and, eventually, through some process of elimination, the IT passes out the bottom for execution. With a universe of possibilities flowing into our finite funnels, there's a limit to what can flow out. Pour too much liquid into a funnel, and you know what happens . . . it overflows. The actions we know are important are displaced by those that seem urgent or are unnecessary. And as we will soon learn, just because something forces its way into your schedule does not make it important.

Organizations can face a similar challenge. Until 2009, Toyota was a paradigm for safety and quality in the automobile industry. The company continued to increase production and market share (a possibility in its funnel it chose to make a priority). In the fall of 2009, however, a series of massive recalls to replace faulty accelerators, floor mats, and engine components severely tarnished the company's image. Toyota's predicament was the result of other priorities forcing one of the most important components of car manufacturing—maintaining high safety and quality standards—to the side.

The narrow neck of a funnel demonstrates the limiting effect of time and resources on our ability to tackle

Let your first IT be to stop.

potential tasks or activities. It's important to remember that only so much can be done to increase the flow of tasks that actually get completed; there are only so many hours in the day. And as quantity increases, quality suffers.

Limitations are not always a hindrance to productivity. A reality check at least keeps some potential but unfeasible items from entering our funnels, and certainly prevents them from becoming IT. When someone expects you to do the impossible and you tell them, "Sorry, but that's not going to happen," you're saying, "You may not drop that into my funnel."

Unfortunately, common sense sometimes doesn't apply. Even with impossible demands, we often say, "I'll see what I can do." Then the task of determining whether the seemingly impossible is really impossible becomes just another item in the funnel.

Ask yourself some questions like these to begin to understand how your funnel got into its current state:

- What criteria or process did I use to determine the tasks that exist in my funnel today? Am I solely reacting to the priorities of others? Are these actions really important to moving my work or life forward?
- Do I see possibilities that have little or no connection to what I view as my priorities right now?
- On what basis did I choose the tasks I performed a few hours ago? Yesterday?

A strong understanding of what you have done to let tasks enter your funnel prepares you for the next step in the process: filtering what makes it through the funnel to become IT.

Evaluating Your Possibilities

You benefit from literal filters every day. Filters in furnaces and water systems keep your environment cleaner and more sanitary than it would otherwise be. As a result, you are healthier and potentially more productive. Your car has a number of filter systems as well. One filters the air that gets into your engine, ensuring it operates at peak efficiency. Another keeps dust and pollen and other aggravating particles from reaching you inside your vehicle. And as a user of the Internet, you benefit from filters that prevent unwanted content from reaching you and your children.

In much the same way, you already employ some mental filters as you determine what possibilities become IT for you. Unfortunately, you may not be nearly as calculating or precise or even as consistent in applying these filters as your car, home heating system, or your computer when it comes to blocking the irrelevant, counterproductive, or even harmful. You might not even be aware that you use filters to organize your time. If so, ask yourself, Why did I choose the clothes

I'm wearing today? or What was my reasoning for starting this task a few hours ago?

While most mechanical filters have a positive purpose, mental filters used to define IT can be positive or negative. Negative filters can come in the form of harmful attitudes that limit you from undertaking tasks for poorly examined reasons, such as assuming you're too old, not educated enough, too poor, or not handsome enough. Negative filters are sometimes the result of other people's influence. These subconscious filters can have a negative impact on your life and can even limit what you might contemplate as IT.

Consider the example of a budding artist who is learning to sketch. Her work is praised by teachers, art lovers, and critics alike. She just has a natural talent that heretofore hasn't required a lot of work. That being said, she is a perfectionist when it comes to completing a piece. Getting something "just right" is not a bad thing, but for her, great is never good enough. Her filter keeps her from finishing her art because getting it just right takes forever; as a result, she truly feels that she isn't talented, despite feedback to the contrary. This then becomes her reality. She won't be a great artist because in her mind she's saying that she will never be a great artist, so why even try?

On the other hand, consider an individual who doesn't have as much natural talent as our first artist. When he was a youth, his artwork would have been

Mental filters used to define IT can be positive or negative.

hanging all over his bedroom, even though it wasn't very good. But he had a different filter (in part, thanks to parents who steadily encouraged him). He had a passion for drawing and proudly showed off his pieces and continually painted, sketched, and sculpted anything that came to mind. Practice and a positive filter truly can make "perfect." Today he owns his own design firm and makes a living as an artist. Oh, the difference a filter can make.

When evaluating your possibilities, be prepared to search out the negative filters you might have in place that prevent you from making room for activities, attitudes, dreams, and goals that would actually enhance or improve your life.

More recognizable are the positive benefits of filters. They might keep you from mental or physical harm. There are moral filters, safety filters, social norms, religious principles, and filters you have developed over time based on your unique wisdom and understanding.

There are also practical filters that can limit or enhance your ability to get things done: the time available at any given moment (e.g., you have thirty minutes to yourself before your next appointment); resources or a lack of resources; your health, energy, moods, and emotions; and, of course, natural laws such as gravity.

*When evaluating your
possibilities, be prepared
to search out the negative
filters you might have
in place that prevent
you from making room
for activities, attitudes,
dreams, and goals that
would actually enhance or
improve your life.*

Using Your Filters

To move forward in your journey to defining IT, work through how best to use your filters. Remember constantly to define IT based on what's practical, because your mind may want to race from the IT for tomorrow to the IT of next year to the IT of your lifetime—and tackling three ITS simultaneously isn't defining IT at all. Treat one period of time as all that matters and filter out other long-range or short-range concerns until you have defined IT. Using this process to your advantage can put you miles ahead of all those individuals who just accept that everything that matters eventually has to be addressed immediately.

Creating filters—and then using them correctly—is an effective way to eliminate the congestion created by all of the things you are struggling to get done. Three filters we will discuss in greater detail are the following:

- your morals, norms, values, ethics, purpose statements, and mission statements
- your responsibilities to others and your roles in a larger community, as well as your personal goals and dreams for the things that you want to achieve in your own life
- your available resources

Your goal with filters is to line up your options to ensure an orderly flow through your funnel so you have clearly defined ITS. Being conscious of your filters ensures that you won't make choices haphazardly.

YOUR MORALS, NORMS, AND VALUES

You already have a set of morals and values either loosely or strongly defined in your head and heart. You act, react, and interact based on these filters. Violation of your core values normally has immediate negative consequences for you. While recalling some of these filters off the top of your head might be easy, you should also write them down—define them in specific detail. Doing so helps ensure that, in a moment of weakness, you don't fail to apply them to your search for IT and also helps you remain accountable.

One approach suggested by Hyrum Smith, a co-founder of FranklinCovey, is to write your values down in the present tense, as if describing the way you are currently, and then review them on a regular basis to test whether those statements about yourself are still valid.

This type of values filter can be seen everywhere, from religious teachings to company mission statements. In our schools, programs and campaigns are constantly reinforcing messages such as "Say no to drugs." Children are encouraged to make a commitment now not to get involved in drugs; that way, when they're presented with temptations in the future, they'll remember that they've already made their choice. As adults, we prepare ourselves in advance with personal and professional ethics so that when we're confronted with the chance to, say, embezzle money or cheat someone, we don't hesitate or debate what's right or wrong.

As a culture, we're now attempting to establish "no texting while driving" as a new norm to cope with a problem that didn't exist several years ago. Insurance companies produce commercials to educate people on the dangers of texting and driving; legislatures establish stiff penalties for those caught texting or phoning when they ought to be paying attention to the road; and cultural leader Oprah Winfrey promotes a "No Phone Zone" pledge. In a relatively short time, as a society we'll establish a new norm that turns a thoughtless act into an unthinkable act, and the possibility of using your phone while driving will be filtered out of consideration as IT.

Making a full list of our filters based on basic ethical commitments and social norms is an arduous task. The list will include everything from how people should be treated to where money should be spent to the types of food we should eat. And efficiently applying every one of these filters to each individual situation we face during the course of a day would be overwhelming.

Yet it's worth being aware of these important filters in our decision making: it's helpful to remind ourselves of our core values. Try making a list of your own. If you struggle with this exercise, ask for help. Those closest to you often have a much more objective view of you than you do, especially because your most characteristic actions are a strong reflection of your moral, social, and ethical filters.

If you ask for feedback on identifying these types of filters, look for patterns in the replies. As a Yiddish proverb concisely puts it, "If one man calls you a donkey, pay him no mind. If two men call you a donkey, get a saddle."

Dr. Spencer Johnson, the coauthor of *The One Minute Manager* and the author of *Who Moved My Cheese?*, is a strong believer in getting feedback from friends, colleagues, and customers. And in analyzing that feedback, he always looks for patterns. When he starts to see a negative pattern, he makes a change; however, if only one person makes a certain comment, he ignores it. Confirmation is a strong indicator of validity.

Applying moral, behavioral, and ethical filters to the flow of possibilities into your funnel won't monumentally reduce the number competing to become your next IT, but affirming that they exist and ensuring that activities that would violate your core tenets don't get into your funnel will reduce headaches and heartache in the future—not to mention preventing those cleanup tasks that will be required after your mistakes. If you or those around you can't say for sure what you wouldn't do to make a sale, win a race, or get ahead in life, then perhaps you've found your IT. As an old country song goes, "You have to stand for something, or you'll fall for anything." Establishing what you stand for and sticking with it, no matter what those around you say or what the rest of the world does, helps to ensure that you always find the IT that's right for you.

What morals, norms, and values that help determine your actions on a regular basis can you identify? Take the time now to write down what sorts of things your own version of this filter will exclude from your funnel.

DOCUMENTED GOALS, RESPONSIBILITIES, ROLES, DREAMS, AND ACHIEVEMENTS

Written goals, what you are "paid to do" at work, and defined responsibilities are all potential components of this type of filter. It also might include the things you are passionate about.

Well-Defined Written Goals

The key word here is *written*. It may be easy for you to say, "I would like to change this . . ." or "If I had time, I would . . ." but those are vague, passing thoughts you're not committed to giving time or energy to (visualize dangling them over your funnel but just not being ready to drop them in). What specific, measurable goals have you captured in writing?

When you were younger, setting goals and achieving them likely was a bigger part of everything you did. You had educational goals, vocational goals, and family goals. As you achieved them and matured, you got into a routine of setting more goals; soon you became overwhelmed with a full funnel—and your daily focus became, essentially, just keeping up. Putting your goals in writing is a good way to make sure that you remember what you've already set as a goal so you'll continue moving toward it, allowing those tasks associated with it to get through your funnel to become IT.

When we speak to groups around the world, we often ask this question: How many of you have goals that you have formally developed and have written down? It is surprising how few people raise their hands. Be one of the few who does more than just dream about what you want to achieve. Take the time right now to formally write down your goals.

What You're Paid for Doing

Because of our work in the training field, we encounter many people who are overburdened at work. They tell us about their current workload, and then mention other important upcoming activities. They then remember all the smaller tasks that dot their plates like peas. We typically allow them to vent for a while before asking, "What are you paid to do?" They rarely respond, "Everything I just told you."

To better define this component, dust off your job description and review your most recent evaluation. Identify four or five things the organization pays you to do—and presumably do well. All the other employment-related items in your funnel can take a number and sit down. If you focus on those essential four or five items and give them enough attention to do them well, the other to-dos may not matter in the larger context. If you're focused on too many nonessential tasks, the result might be that your true ITS— the four or five tasks you were hired to do—don't get completed, or at least don't get completed as well as they might be if you gave them your all.

This strategy also applies to the other roles in your life. What are the three or four things that you can do as a parent, neighbor, volunteer, baseball coach, Sunday school teacher, gardener, son-in-law, dancer, and so on, that make the greatest impact? Three or four key things are doable. Ten or twelve items can be overwhelming.

The business guru and former General Electric CEO Jack Welch once said, "If someone tells me, 'I'm working ninety hours a week,' I tell them, 'You're doing something terribly wrong. I go skiing on the weekend. I go out with my buddies on Friday . . .' Make a list of twenty things that make your work ninety hours, and ten of them have to be nonsense."

Passions

Ask yourself, What do I enjoy doing? You might want to reflect on the times in your life when you've been most engaged and energized. What projects, plans, or tasks are most likely to make you feel motivated? On the other hand, do you sometimes feel there's a motivational void—something missing—related to what you're expected to do? Maybe that's because you've lost your passion for that kind of project—or you've succeeded in putting what was once an inspiring dream or goal aside to make room for the many urgent (but not necessarily important) chores demanding your attention. If you look at all of the possibilities crowding your funnel and realize none of them invokes even a middling level of passion within you, you might want to ask yourself why you let them into your funnel in the first place.

Take some time now to write down what makes something passionately important for you. Review the list often to remind yourself there's more to life than merely slogging from one chore to the next, and add to the list as you develop new passions.

THE RESOURCES AVAILABLE, YOUR PRIORITIES,
AND DISTINGUISHING WHAT IS "BEST" FROM
WHAT IS "GOOD"

When you're shopping for furnace filters or automotive filters, you no doubt notice they come in three categories: basic or economy grade, midrange, and premium. The higher-quality filters are more expensive, but they usually provide compensating benefit. If the filter is crucial—protecting your engine from failure, assuring the health of your family, maintaining the livability of your home—there often can be a hidden cost over time in purchasing merely a "good" filter rather than one of the highest quality.

It's a familiar dilemma: any number of options are passable, good enough to fit the requirements of the moment, but settling for one of them will prove to be unsatisfactory in the long run. At work, for example, you might take care of the crises and urgent tasks, but the exceptional ideas and breakthrough projects that could really move your organization ahead of the competition are rarely given serious attention. At home, your relationship with your children or spouse is "fine," but you know there are so many wasted sunny weekends, postponed outings, rushed holidays, and routine evenings that the dream you once had of an ideal family life seems to have faded into nothing more than memory. Most of us know what it's like to push aside our most cherished dreams, plans, and goals—those that, if realized, might restore much-needed passion and energy to our lives—until "maybe someday."

What if you applied the "best" filter to every possibility in your funnel, asking yourself, What is the most

Important Thing I could be doing to accomplish what matters most? Over time, you're likely to see a noticeable increase in the quality of your work and your personal life, because you've gradually aligned your efforts with the best possible outcome.

The list of possibilities in your funnel that are candidates for IT should be growing shorter by now, but keep in mind that the outlet of your funnel is very narrow. Generally, the key to refining your choices to the optimum IT is to be proactive and strategic rather than reactive and tactical. Although it may be easier to choose whatever is most convenient, or requires the least time and effort, or makes you look busy, or is fun or entertaining, if they're just time fillers rather than the most Important Things you could be focusing on, you still need to refine your decision-making process.

To get to what is *most* important, you might need to employ some "tactical prioritization." The filters we discussed earlier were generally strategic; with a tactical filter, you're looking at the immediate situation and environment around you and making frequent adjustments. Like a commander in the field rather than a general back at HQ, you're reviewing your resources at hand and deploying them to achieve the best result possible given real-world limitations. To "appreciate" (in the military sense) those limitations, take time to ask yourself these questions:

- What deadlines are approaching?
- As an employee, what priorities are set for me (either documented or implied) by my organization?
- Does the current situation present problems and opportunities for me personally or professionally? If so, what are they?
- How much time do I have to devote to the ideal goal right now?
- What is the one action I could take today— this hour—that would get me an inch closer to accomplishing my most important goals?
- What is the one obstacle that needs to be removed before I can make progress toward the ultimate goal?
- What is the one conversation or discussion I should have with someone that would help me (and possibly others) clarify what is most important?
- What information do I possess already that can move me forward just enough to build some momentum?

Apply enough tactical filters at this point and you're certain to make progress toward IT. But before you celebrate (that comes in chapter 7, After Accomplishing It), bear in mind that you're working against the impulse to focus on the merely urgent. Remember, urgent does not necessarily mean important. A phone call from a potential vendor might be urgent (it's a ringing phone), but it might not be as important as working on next year's budget, which is due Friday. On the other hand, answering a callback from a vendor who's located the hard-to-find replacement part needed to get a crucial machine operational again would be both urgent and important. Something that demands your attention may be urgent, but it's important only if it serves the strategic goal you've set as IT.

Using filters like those we've just discussed removes ones of convenience, laziness, procrastination, corruption, fear, as well as a hundred others, and replaces them with fulfilled dreams, achieved goals, and completed tasks that bring happiness, contentment, and success.

Commit to selecting your goals carefully and consciously and then choosing courses of action that align with the goal. Invest the time it takes to identify fully what is most important in the long run and also what is most important right now to move you in the straightest possible line toward that goal.

Prioritizing Your Filters When Conflicts Arise

Given that you'll need numerous filters to thin out all the possibilities competing for your attention and energy, prioritizing those filters can be a necessity, especially when they seem to conflict with one another.

When conflicts arise, you may need to reexamine your filters, set some aside—not, of course, those representing your core values—and add others.

Let's say two of Julia's filters are being a good spouse/partner and being a responsible employee. Then one day she realizes she has an important business trip scheduled on her wedding anniversary. What does she do? Which of several possible courses of action does she choose as IT? Prioritizing one of her filters over the other might help her resolve the conflict. She might tell the client she is unavailable or negotiate with her spouse about when they celebrate their anniversary.

FAILURE TO FOCUS ON THE RIGHT IT AT THE RIGHT TIME (USE OF THE WRONG FILTERS; E.G., IMMEDIATE GRATIFICATION, CONVENIENCE)

You may have neglected working toward a goal for too long, and, as a result, it has now become urgent as well as important. Perhaps you were prioritizing your options based on what could be crossed off your list quickly, and the long-deferred objective demanded more time than you felt was available. As we described earlier, you've made the false step of tackling the easiest task first rather than starting on the more important but difficult project. Or you might have given in to the merely urgent situations—the squeakiest wheels—

when giving attention to a less pressing but more important goal might have made for a better outcome.

A good example is getting the education necessary for a future career. Some high school graduates find themselves making money right after graduation and enjoying the freedom that earning money provides. After several years go by, they then realize that they need to enhance their education in order to compete with new hires or to qualify for advancement. The dilemma is that they now have bills to pay and possibly a family to support, making it much more difficult to earn a college degree.

If you find yourself in a similar situation, ask yourself, What can I do now that will make it easier to work on IT tomorrow? Jarring yourself with the realization that delaying work on IT, even for another day, will have a greater impact on you (and possibly others) further off in the future is sometimes enough to get you to take the first steps in the right direction.

Filters can also help you develop the will to say no to everything else to protect IT.

You may have visualized your funnel on paper, deployed your filters, ejected the less-important options, defined your IT, and now you feel that the process is complete—all that remains is executing IT. Before congratulating yourself, however, keep in mind that during every step of the way toward completing IT, there will be a constant stream of options pouring into

There will always be more possibilities in your funnel than you can ever hope to complete. Ultimately, you will have to say no to the possibilities recommended by others that don't align with your filters.

your funnel and clamoring for attention—more, in fact, than you can ever accommodate.

Let's go back to the vacant lot example. Once you begin cleaning your lot and building on it, not everyone will be happy. The neighbors who dumped their trash and grass clippings on your lot will be frustrated that they'll now have to find another dumping ground. Adjacent landowners may be upset because the neat and healthy appearance of your lot is making theirs look tacky in comparison. Be prepared: you might know the best use of your own resources, but others will want to appropriate them for their own purposes. You might even be doing such a superb job of tending your lot that others will want you to look after theirs. At some point, you'll have to say no to the options strongly favored by others that don't align with your filters.

Todd recalls a time when saying no to a busy work schedule was required to focus on the right IT. He was invited to attend an "author's tea" at the elementary school where his daughter, along with her classmates, would read aloud an illustrated story each had been working on for quite some time. His initial reaction was, "How can I do this? I have so much to do at work and will need to rearrange my schedule." But the morning before the big event, as he talked with his daughter, he knew that it was very important to her for him to be there. So he rearranged his schedule and redefined IT for his morning.

Parents gathered together in the classroom, were greeted by their excited children, and were assigned to sit in circles with five or six students. In the circle where Todd and his daughter sat were six students but only five guests. One student sat alone. Tears streamed down the little boy's face as he confided that no one in his family could make it that day. One concerned mother quickly adjusted the seating in the circle so she could put her arm around the boy as he quietly attempted to read his story. Todd will never forget the face of that child. He also vividly remembers how his daughter leaned in to him and whispered, "Thanks, Dad, for coming." Choosing your IT wisely and being willing to say no to things that matter and instead saying yes to that which matters most can make a difference. Scope creep is a common challenge in many organizations and a prime example of the need to have the right filters in place. You are assigned a project with specific outcomes, but as you begin to complete each element of the project successfully, the scope is broadened, more tasks are added, and it's now grown beyond you or your team's ability to accomplish with any degree of excellence. Having (and communicating) the filters that prompt you to resist adding new tasks to this project is critical.

An insightful quote by Jon Kabat-Zinn, an advocate of mindfulness meditation, may help you see the importance of saying no: "Saying 'yes' to more things than we can actually manage to be present for with integrity and ease of being is in effect saying 'no' to all those things and people and places we have already said 'yes' to."

Once you have zeroed in on IT through the use of your filters, allowing others who have little (if any) understanding of all of those factors to twist and shape your workday and everyday life into something else would be absurd. But it does happen, doesn't it?

Here are a few suggestions to help you develop the mental and emotional backbone to say no to the things that simply shouldn't make your IT list:

- Avoid giving an emotional yes when you would give a logical no. Before saying yes to any obligation or commitment, ask yourself what filters you are using to determine if this option should become IT. Do they include something as questionable as not wanting to appear less than superhuman? Also reflect on the other possibilities you have in your funnel. Could saying yes to this option cause you to say no to alternatives that are more closely aligned with your other filters? If the situation allows, reserve for yourself some time for reflection before you give a definite answer. Unless the decision to say yes involves someone's personal safety or well-being—the guy next to you is on fire and you need to douse him with water—stopping to engage your filters will result in a better decision for everyone involved.

- Start with "no." Too often, people start with "yes" and then have to figure out how to make the commitment work with an already overtaxed schedule. Beginning with no may force you to apply your filters to determine whether you actually could say yes, while simply starting with the affirmative response moves the item (often too quickly) to the bottom of your funnel.
- Keep in mind the Law of Previous ITs: Just because IT was an IT before doesn't mean that IT should be an IT today. There are always new possibilities entering your funnel. In order to say yes to something new, you may need to say no to something you are currently doing. Remember to prioritize by good, better, and best. If you have an opportunity to complete something that is "best," you may have to say no to something that is merely "good."
- Communicate IT to others. The importance of this concept will be covered in greater detail in a later chapter, but at this point just keep in mind that if people know what you are working on and why it's important to you, they may be less likely to ask you to take on something else.

Law of Previous Its: Just because IT was an IT before doesn't mean that IT should be an IT today.

Determining the It of the Moment

Don't let the present moment be overlooked. You may not need to revisit the five steps in this chapter every fifteen minutes, but frequently asking yourself about the filters you're using (or should use) to choose the next option helps ensure that you stay on course to accomplish IT at every moment.

Your Defining Moment

Once you have resisted the chaos created by too many possibilities and have made choices that will move you forward both professionally and personally, you hold in your mind (and in your hand, if you've written IT down) the most important action to take, and now it's time to get IT done. You probably recognize that defining IT is no small task. If it were, you would have no need for this book!

President Harry S. Truman had a famous sign on his desk: THE BUCK STOPS HERE. That expression dates from the mid-1800s, when in a poker game a piece of buckshot or other object was passed around to remind the players whose turn it was to be the next dealer.

Certainly, the one person who doesn't have the option of passing the buck to someone else is the president. But what Truman was also saying about his presidency was, "I will take responsibility for any issue that arrives at my desk. I will not pass it on to someone else."

You have accepted the "buck" by defining IT for yourself. The question now may be, Do I really believe I can accomplish IT?

Chapter 3

*Believing I*T

YOU KNOW WHAT YOU BELIEVE ABOUT **IT**, BUT DO YOU BELIEVE WHAT YOU KNOW?

In chapter 1, What Is IT?, we introduced the Law of the Vacant Lot: if you don't plan for and act on how you will use a vacant lot, nature or squatters will move in and make those decisions for you. At this point in your journey to accomplish IT, your "lot" may not have changed. The things you've built on your lot—or allowed others to build—are still there. Renovating, remodeling, or simply clearing away some of these unwelcome "improvements" from your lot takes time and energy—and the motivation to stay focused on taking action on IT is critical at this point. Believing in IT provides the motivation needed to stay the course.

The actual process of defining IT has probably already stirred some positive emotions such as excitement, energy, determination, and a desire to accomplish IT. Unfortunately, as time passes, those positive emotions often give way to doubt, fatigue, and frustration. How do you sustain your belief, energy, and excitement in the IT you plan to accomplish?

Your confidence and determination become more essential as the scale of IT increases. Positive feedback may not be as immediate and frequent, and the resources required are likely to be much greater with a long-term or complex IT. More modest ITS typically don't require a significant amount of mental or emotional "cheering on" to reach the finish line. Regardless of the scale of your IT, a firm conviction that IT can be done is crucial to staying on track.

You can reinforce this conviction by doing the following:

• Confirm your commitment of time and energy.
• Engage your heart.
• Remove the "Four N's."
• Visualize the eventual benefits.

Confirm Your Commitment of Time and Energy to Make It Successful

One reason your vacant lot became overrun with so many unwelcome impositions might be a lack of commitment to focusing on what is most important to you.

Believing in IT is the motivation needed to stay the course.

Any number of factors could have contributed to the loss of control of your own real estate: unfavorable economic conditions, a new job or position, poor supervision, lack of support from those around you . . . Setbacks may have been acceptable in the past or in special cases, but what about now? Ask yourself, Am I at last ready to commit to accomplishing IT?

Vince Lombardi once said, "The difference between a successful person and others is not a lack of strength, not a lack of knowledge, but rather a lack of will." Are you ready to commit the time and energy necessary to make IT successful? Do you have the will? It's important to remember that there's a solid reason IT made it into your funnel, through your filters, and onto your schedule: IT is important to you.

Because we're published authors, we're frequently approached by individuals who say, "Oh, I want to write a book." They proceed to give us the premise and their goals for the project. You can see the excitement in their face and hear the enthusiasm in their words. When they ask for advice, one of our first comments is simply "Start writing." At that point much of their energy toward the project disappears. They just don't have the will to get up early, stay up late, or make writing a priority.

Jones has a daughter who's an avid runner. Her favorite event is the half marathon. Some time ago, a friend of hers told her that she, too, would like to run a 13.1-mile course. But in the next sentence the friend exposed her true level of commitment when she added, "But I'm not willing to put in all the miles and miles of training to get ready for it." Whatever IT is, IT rarely gets accomplished without the willpower to make IT a reality.

Engage Your Heart, Not Just Your Head

An old saying goes, "Most people fail because they never make the journey of eighteen inches—the distance from the head to the heart." Without the involvement of your heart, you might quickly be overwhelmed with countless reasons why you can't possibly succeed at IT. You start looking around at all of the data that indicates failure is likely. You look at the unsuccessful experiences of others and justify your worst-case expectations with thoughts like, "If they couldn't do it, as talented as they are, there's little chance I'll be able to do IT." Or it could just come down to being overwhelmed with all of the other commitments bearing down on you, which leads to despair or, its cousin, apathy. It's in those moments of self-doubt that your heart—your inner drive—can make all the difference and help you stay the course.

The Olympic Games offer wonderful stories of individuals and teams whose heart and passion carry them far beyond the performance levels of even top-notch

Whatever IT is, IT rarely gets accomplished without the willpower to make IT a reality.

athletes. While physical abilities certainly are important, the heart can tip the balance between merely impressive and downright legendary accomplishments. The record of the US Olympic downhill skier Bode Miller is a good example. In the 2006 Winter Games in Turin, Italy, Miller was at the top of his game physically and was expected to win multiple medals in the downhill, slalom, and super-G. Yet he left Turin with none. He seemed emotionally distant from the Games . . . at least the competition part of the Games. Sally Jenkins, a sportswriter for the *Washington Post*, wrote, "Miller is the biggest disappointment in the Winter Olympics, not because of the way he skied the mountain, but the way he acted at the bottom of it. . . . The point is that he acted like he didn't try, and didn't care."[1]

We saw a very different Bode Miller in the 2010 Vancouver Games. He admitted that he was not in peak physical condition, but mentally and emotionally he pushed himself to win a gold medal in the super combined, a silver medal in the super-G, and a bronze medal in the downhill. When asked about how he felt about winning the gold medal, he is quoted as saying, "If I had won it in a way I wasn't excited about or wasn't proud of, I would have resented the gold medal in a way."[2] His emotional focus was even more clear when he later described how he raced: "I let all that stuff go and raced like I was a little kid."[3]

Another example is the courage and drive of the Canadian figure skater Joannie Rochette, whose mother died from a heart attack two days before Joannie was scheduled to compete in the 2010 Winter Olympics. Forty-eight hours after being awakened by her father with the terrible news, Joannie skated her short program perfectly. After her performance, Skate Canada's high-performance director Mike Slipchuk said, "When she took to the ice, she looked like the Joannie we've known and grown with. She was as good as she's been all year. That's just a testament to her, to be able to get herself in the right frame of mind, in the moment, and do it."[4]

Joannie channeled her emotions about her mother into the performance of a lifetime—even as she was coping with raw, aching loss. Her heart and passion drove her forward to win a bronze medal in women's figure skating after another amazing performance in the long skate just two days later.

You don't have to be an Olympic athlete to dig deep and be passionate and emotional about achieving your goals; it's often just as true of businesspeople. Professionals with Ivy League degrees and exceptional intelligence nonetheless sometimes fail because they lack passion, while people with average intelligence and unremarkable educations manage to succeed because they bring to their work a positive attitude and an excitement that rallies those around them. Some examples include these:

- Andrew Carnegie, industrialist and philanthropist.
  Carnegie started working as a bobbin boy in a
  textile mill at the age of thirteen (after dropping
  out of school) and eventually came to dominate the
  American steel industry. By the time of his death,
  he had given away more than $4 billion (in current
  dollars).
- Debbi Fields, founder of Mrs. Fields Cookies. Fields
  founded the company as a twenty-one-year-old
  mother with no business experience.
- Whoopi Goldberg, Oscar-winning actress,
  comedienne, and talk-show host. Goldberg battled
  drug addiction and dropped out of high school.
  After overcoming the addiction, she worked as
  a bricklayer and trained as a beautician before
  becoming a successful comedienne.
- Mark Zuckerberg, founder of Facebook. Zuckerberg
  developed the social media platform along with
  Dustin Moskovitz, Chris Hughes, and Eduardo
  Saverin, and launched it from his dorm room in
  February 2004. He later dropped out of Harvard
  University.[5]

And how about the will and drive of J. K. Rowling,
the bestselling author of the Harry Potter series? A
few years out of college, divorced, unemployed, and
raising her daughter as a single mother, Rowling
thought of herself as "the biggest failure I knew" and

contemplated suicide. Instead, she "began to direct all my energy to finishing the only work that mattered to me. Had I really succeeded at anything else, I might never have found the determination to succeed in the one area where I truly belonged."[6] She is now one of the few novelists in history to become a billionaire.

What passion burns within you? Is your focus and the activities that you are engaged in aligned with that passion? If the thought of accomplishing IT does not stir something deep within you, we suggest that you return to chapter 2, Defining IT, to reread the section titled Using Your Filters.

Remove the Four N's

Actually, it's more like one "N" with four parts. The N? Negativity. To maintain your belief in IT, you must eliminate as much as possible of the negativity you're likely to encounter. Working on your vacant lot is difficult enough without neighbors peering over the fence and telling you that you're doing it all wrong and should give up.

NEGATIVE THOUGHTS

If you're a parent or have ever worked with small children, you know how impossible it can be to get them to do something once they convince themselves they can't do it. Inside their budding minds their imaginations conjure up a million reasons why they cannot be successful at something. You ask them why they won't even try, they give you a reason, you remove the obstacle (mental or physical), and then they still won't attempt it. You show them how it can be accomplished, and they don't believe you. Try as you might, you won't get them to accept any new attitudes or behaviors as long as their minds are flooded with those negative "can't do" thoughts.

Even for adults, slipping back into that attitude can be easy to do, although the challenge is unlikely to be about riding a bike or swimming or entering a dark room. If you're hesitating to believe in IT, you probably have allowed your mind to be flooded with those same paralyzing negative thoughts. Worse, you're encouraging your mind to turn those negative possibilities into reality. Hypochondriacs are known to experience the exact symptoms of the illness they profess to have. Their constant mental dwelling on "what could be" leads their bodies to exhibit physical symptoms. Just as your body is protected when it enjoys a nourishing, balanced diet, your mental well-being depends on being fed a diet of nurturing, positive thoughts.

The most prevalent negative thoughts typically stem from fear. As Brian Tracy, the author of *Eat That Frog*, writes, "The biggest enemies we have to overcome on the road to success are not a lack of ability and a lack of opportunity, but fears of failure and rejection and the doubts that they trigger." As adults, we don't often like to talk about our fears, but that doesn't mean they're any less real. The more we allow them to take up residence in our thinking, the faster they grow, consuming our thought processes and inhibiting our progress toward success. It's important to remember that successful people are not exempt from fear; rather, they have the courage to set their fears aside, channel positive thoughts of success, and move forward with determination.

To deflect negative thoughts or fears, try to recognize them the moment they enter your mind and immediately work to counter them with positive "can do" thoughts. Try reciting a quote that has meaning to you, or reflect on times when you've undertaken something much more difficult than the problem at hand and were able to accomplish it. Instead of feeling overwhelmed by the vastness of the task before you, set about accomplishing a small part of the task that could be completed almost immediately. When you've accomplished this smaller IT, you'll have reminded yourself that you can succeed.

Your negative thoughts may be a result of your memory of past mistakes, deterring you from taking a similar route in the here and now. There are many examples of people who managed to put their failures behind them, undertook a new task, and successfully completed it. Harland Sanders, or "Colonel Sanders" as much of the world knew him, developed a now-famous fried-chicken recipe, but he was rejected over a thousand times before Pete Harman in South Salt Lake City was willing to take a chance with him. They opened the first Kentucky Fried Chicken in 1952.[7]

Forgiving yourself and others for past mistakes or failures can be a critical step in replacing negative thoughts with positive actions. Don't dwell on the past. Learn from it, forgive yourself and others, and then move forward.

To further deal with your fears surrounding IT, name the fear and seek to render it powerless. If it's the fear of failure, find someone who has accomplished something similar and learn from him or her. If it's the fear of risking financial loss, counter it with rational measures to minimize the potential downside— what financial managers call "hedges." If it's the fear of not having enough time, go back and review your filters. Also think about other items on your schedule that you could delegate, delay, or delete to make more room for IT.

Another approach is to focus on reasonable fears that would drive you toward working on IT. Being offered a leadership role on a new initiative at work may conjure up many fears that might hold you back. But the fear of producing an unsatisfactory (to your boss or, more important, to yourself) result, missing an

Forgiving yourself and others for past mistakes or failures can be a critical step in replacing negative thoughts with positive actions. Don't dwell on the past. Learn from it, forgive yourself and others, and then move forward.

opportunity for advancement, or becoming stagnant in your current responsibilities may be just the catalysts to push you forward. The key here is to focus on completing IT. The more your capacity is occupied with positive thoughts and possibilities, the less room there will be for your mind to engage in negative thinking.

Think back to the example of helping a child accomplish something unfamiliar and scary, like riding a bike or performing in a school play. When teaching a child to ride a bike without training wheels, you don't simply give her a push and say, "Good luck!" Instead, you create a secure, nonthreatening situation where the child can enjoy a string of small successes that gradually replace "I can't" fears with "I already have" memories. Soon you're running to keep up with her as she rides away.

NEGATIVE ATTITUDES

There probably are more books written about the importance of a positive attitude than any other self-help subject. If it's not the focus of the entire book, there are usually at least chapters or pages devoted to the subject. Why? Because people continually have to be reminded of the need to stay positive. Consider what the German poet and philosopher Goethe wrote: "All truly wise thoughts have been thought already thousands of times. To make them truly yours, you must think them over again honestly, until they take root in your personal experience."

Stories of people who accomplish seemingly impossible feats of endurance or strength when they find themselves in life-or-death situations are regularly reported in the news: soldiers who continue fighting after being shot multiple times, firefighters who battle wildfires for days without sleep. Then there are the many unsung heroes—single mothers who work two jobs while raising children, the parents of children with disabilities who work tirelessly to ensure their sons or daughters have every opportunity to reach their full potential. The difference between such people and the average person is often their steadfast positive attitude. The possibility of failure simply doesn't enter their minds.

While it may seem impossible to reach the exceptional level of the individuals just described, consider times in the past when you also harnessed the power of a positive attitude. Think about preparing for an upcoming vacation. You want to get everything in order before you leave, and therefore you work harder than usual, accomplishing much more than you would in a typical day or an average week. How about preparing for a certification exam or a major test in school? No doubt you pushed yourself beyond what you thought you were capable of doing. You stretched your mental muscles and achieved your goal.

The mental strength needed to accomplish IT is available to you if you have a positive attitude. Reflect on yours for a moment. Is it likely to increase your chances of succeeding at IT? Or does your attitude encourage fear, negative self-talk, and worry that paralyzes you and prevents you from taking action? Do you instead focus on easy or convenient tasks that merely fill time and make you look busy?

The legendary football coach Lou Holtz knows a few things about attitude and motivation. Several times in his successful career, he was called upon to turn a struggling football program into a winner.

In 1986 Holtz accepted the head coaching job at the University of Notre Dame, taking them from a 5–6 record to an appearance in the Cotton Bowl Classic; in his third season with them, the team won all eleven of its regular-season games. They then went on to defeat the third-ranked West Virginia Mountaineers in the Fiesta Bowl, claiming the NCAA Division I FBS National Football Championship.

Holtz is the only college football coach to lead six different programs to bowl games, and the only coach to guide four different programs to final top-twenty rankings. He is known for his ability not only to inspire players, but also to inspire audiences as a motivational speaker. One of his best-known quotes is, "Ability is what you're capable of doing. Motivation determines what you do. Attitude determines how well you do it."

Reflect on your attitude for a moment. Is it likely to increase your chances of succeeding at IT?

Which way is your attitude moving you: toward success or away from it? Consider these suggestions to move it in the right direction (or keep it there):

- Surround yourself with positive reminders. The Successories company (you know the one— they market posters with positive, uplifting, inspirational messages, like "Customer service is not a department—it's an attitude") has achieved remarkable success over the years by helping other organizations motivate their teams. Walk through the halls and break rooms of almost any successful company, and you're likely to see familiar Successories banners and framed pictures with images and quotations that offer employees positive reminders of their own capabilities. You don't have to use theirs, however. Come up with ones of your own that are meaningful and that offer a quick opportunity for you to check your attitude. Jones keeps a list on his phone that he can review at any moment.
- Listen to a successful coach, artist, athlete, parent, or anyone who has achieved a level of excellence in his or her field, and you're likely to hear a phrase or sentence that has helped him or her stay focused on what was most important.
- Memorize a quotation or coin a phrase of your own that you can repeat over and over again until you feel it increase your level of motivation, courage, and

willingness to work on IT. Even repeating "I can do IT" can make a big difference in your performance, as we discussed earlier in the section on positive thoughts. When Todd is faced with a challenge or something he's anxious or fearful about, he repeats this line from William Shakespeare's *Measure for Measure*: "Our doubts are traitors and make us lose the good we oft might win by fearing to attempt." Jones has a motivational mantra of his own, something Dr. Phil McGraw once said: "Winners do the things losers don't want to do."

NEGATIVE PEOPLE

In his book *Margin*, Dr. Richard Swenson talks about three types of people all of us encounter in our lives: fillers, drainers, and the people who just sit there. Fillers are those amazing people who pour confidence into you, making you feel better about yourself and your goals. A conversation with a filler leaves you more motivated than ever to be your best. Drainers, on the other hand, siphon off any positive energy you have, convincing you that you can never accomplish much more than you already have, which was most likely a fluke. Although you might know to resist a drainer, telling yourself, "I don't want to be like him," hang out with a drainer long enough and you, too, are likely to wear a big *D* on your shirt someday.

Then there are the people who just sit there . . . Well, what else can be said about them? While they may appear to be neither encouraging nor discouraging, they're often as much a hindrance as a drainer because they don't offer any support. They don't stand in your way, but they don't encourage you to keep going, either. And as we explained earlier, you want people in your life who support you in your quest to accomplish IT.

"But my job requires me to work with lots of drainers!" you protest. Fair enough . . . We can't choose our coworkers. But what do you do when you do have a choice? Do you seek out mentors and fillers? Or do you gravitate toward the drainers and sitters?

If you're about to undertake a major IT, it's important to surround yourself with lots of fillers and to keep them close. You're going to need them, especially if you anticipate challenges or setbacks (and what worthy IT doesn't have those?). Reach out to positive people who believe in you and in your ability to accomplish IT.

While our focus thus far has been on *your* IT, don't miss an opportunity to be a filler for others as they work on *their* IT. You encourage people to help you when you need help with IT if they know they can expect the same of you.

NEGATIVE CIRCUMSTANCES

There's a principle in classical physics called the Law of Conservation of Matter that states that matter can be neither created nor destroyed—it just changes form. Like matter, our thoughts also seem to be indestructible: we can't annihilate negative thoughts, but we can replace them with something positive. Making the commitment to turn around a negative attitude is a step in the right direction, but unless we actively cultivate a positive attitude in its place, something equally nasty is likely to sprout up uninvited. (Remember our Law of the Vacant Lot.)

You might want to eliminate a counterproductive work or personal habit, but if you don't replace the negative habit with a positive one, another bad habit is likely to take its place. Similarly, you can set about minimizing your exposure to negative people, but unless you replace those relationships with positive ones, you could simply end up alone—with no more support than you had before.

Jones's eating habits provide a good example of how to deal with negative circumstances, and the need to replace negative ones with more positive ones.

In the past, Jones had a rather bad habit of overindulging in airport food when he traveled. He could tell you the best places to eat or where to satisfy a sweet tooth in almost any airport. When he began focusing more proactively on his health (and his waistline), he chose to refrain from unhealthy airport food. It sounded like a noble enough plan, but he soon encountered another problem: his frugal nature made him unwilling to pay a premium for healthy options or snacks. He was able to fight off his craving for junk food, but he hadn't found a way to satisfy his hunger with healthy food . . . until recently. Now he tucks a bag of almonds and a few cereal bars in his pockets when he travels. If he passes a food vendor in an airport and swoons at the aroma of greasy fries or cinnamon buns dripping with sugar glaze, all he has to do is reach into his travel bag to find the immediate gratification of a healthy alternative—and they cost much less than if he had purchased them at an airport store.

Removing negativity is critical to maintaining our commitment to IT, but it requires replacing the negatives with something more positive.

A strong effort is sometimes necessary to replace negative factors with positive ones. They are often deeply ingrained attitudes or routines. Your vacant or neglected lot may have become overgrown with uninvited weeds and cluttered with someone else's rubbish because you were simply too busy to pay attention to what was gradually happening. To minimize opportunities for negativity to take up residence on your vacant lot in the future, try to anticipate the kind of negative influences you're prone to. Be as specific and tangible as possible, taking note of situations in the past where negativity has taken hold over you. You can then recognize such situations well in advance and take steps to avoid negativity when you see it coming. You may have a coworker who brings out the worst in you because of his negative attitude. When you know you will be working with this person, remind yourself that he shouldn't control your thoughts or attitude. Make a mental note of the types or topics that normally set you off and do everything possible to avoid those areas for discussion. Plan ways to redirect the conversation if you sense the hair on the back of your neck beginning to rise. If all else fails, try the direct approach. Schedule a time to talk with your coworker and discuss your feelings about his negative attitude. Be willing to listen, and together come to a solution that could help you both.

Though cataloging negative traps in your past doesn't guarantee you won't fall into the next one, being able to recognize the hungry wolf of negativity even when it comes disguised as a sheep will help you fend off its advances.

Visualize the Benefits of Working On and Accomplishing It

Once you master the skill of keeping a positive attitude, you'll naturally begin looking forward to the benefits of accomplishing IT: "We're going to get this marketing plan implemented, and then I can have my life back!" Visualize those benefits—"When this trade show is over, I'm going to spend a week lying on a beach sipping drinks with little pink umbrellas in them!"—and keep those images in the forefront of your mind where you can see them often. Think through your typical day and reflect on what will be different after you've accomplished IT. As part of your positive motivation for working on IT, don't forget to ask yourself, How will things be better for those around me when IT is accomplished?

Find words to describe what your situation will be like when you accomplish IT. Stick with positive words like *clarity, peace, fulfillment,* and *relief.*

Draw on the power of visualization. An athlete imagines the feeling of having a gold medal placed around her neck or the sound of the crowd cheering as she scores the winning points. Maybe you'll imagine your expression of happiness as you open your paycheck to find a handsome bonus as a result of accomplishing IT, or the smile on your face as you watch your CEO hang a photo of you on the Employee of the Month wall, or your sigh of pleasure when you discover a thank-you card someone has left on your desk. Creating positive pictures of the end result provides motivation to develop the plan to accomplish IT.

If the effort ahead to accomplish IT seems like nothing but blood, sweat, and tears, reflect on your own life

Visualize the benefits of working on and accomplishing IT.

experiences for a moment. While progress often isn't easy, the benefits of your work don't start only when you've finished IT. Often they start immediately. If you make the decision that your IT is to lose twenty pounds, you won't have to wait until you've lost all twenty pounds to experience the benefit; the moment you discover that healthy food can also be delicious will be rewarding in and of itself. If you make the decision to get your master's degree, you won't have to wait until the diploma is in your hands (and the money is out of your wallet) to experience stimulation and a sense of accomplishment. Just interacting with other individuals who are passionate about their careers and striving for growth may be a benefit you experience from the outset.

A secondary benefit that may arise from your work on IT is that you can more clearly plan your next IT. Let's say IT for you is to have a conversation you expect to be uncomfortable but that could have positive implications for the future. You may not like IT, but taking action might point you in the direction to go next as a result of completing IT. If IT is developing a budget, then once you've completed IT, you have the information you need to plan purchases for yourself for the coming months.

A Final Word About Believing in I<small>T</small>

As friends and business partners, Jones and Todd have many things in common. One is that their children are all girls. They both are the lone males in their households (except for the dogs . . . and a cat at Jones's house). They have endured (and enjoyed) all of the tea parties, dress-up moments, and other inevitable rites of passage that come with having daughters, including the movies about princesses and those who secretly know themselves to be princesses forced by plot twists to live with boring commoners pretending to be parents. In the midst of one of those story lines came a passage perfect for describing IT. In *The Princess Diaries*, Mia's father writes to his daughter about the need for her to believe in herself. He begins by quoting the mystic, philosopher, and former rock-band manager Ambrose Redmoon. He writes: "Courage is not the absence of fear, but rather the judgment that something else is more important than fear. The brave may not live forever, but the cautious do not live at all."

Believing you can accomplish what is most important to you doesn't mean you won't have anxiety about the decision or fears about the outcome. It simply means that you know that the joy, satisfaction, peace, or reward that comes from accomplishing IT is worth far more than merely allowing the possibility to stay indefinitely in your funnel or get forced out by a million other things. Allow yourself to make the journey. Believe IT can happen, and take the next step . . . communicate IT to others.

Chapter 4

Communicating It

MANY ARE THE PLANS AND FEW ARE THE
SUCCESSES OF THE PERSON WHO HAS DREAMS
BUT TELLS NO ONE.

Let's suppose we dropped by your workplace today to offer our support for your journey to accomplish IT. Before we talk with you, we're going to interview your boss and everyone you've worked with during the past week. We'll ask them one question: What's IT for [your name] right now? What would they tell us? Would the IT they describe have any resemblance to the IT you're actually working on?

Later, you invite us to meet your family. When we arrive at your home, a phone call takes you away for a moment. In your absence, we conduct the same interview with each family member: What's IT for [your name] right now? How would those in your family respond?

Then we leave your home and stop at a local restaurant for a bite to eat. Several of the people there know you; some are your close friends. What a coincidence! We conduct one final series of interviews, asking the same question. What will these people tell us?

While the exercise described above is a bit unrealistic, communicating the most Important Thing you're working on to those who have (or should have) a great interest in ITS success can be a crucial part of the process. We do not work, rest, live, or die in isolation. Communicating your values, goals, and activities builds a framework of support that helps you in your quest to achieve what is most important to you. In this chapter, we will discuss why it's important to communicate IT to others and the benefits that communication brings about.

Why You Should Communicate It

There are numerous examples of why it's important to communicate IT. Here are a few.

SO OTHERS CAN SUPPORT YOU

Communicating IT with others is an effective way to gain support. Unless you have nothing but enemies (if so, we have an idea for your next IT), communicating a goal; project plans; or an intended change in attitude, work habits, or behavior allows other people to assist you when you need help. They can provide resources, serve as a sounding board, give encouragement, or even offer ideas. Your support team (whether at home or at work) can even choose to change its own habits or behaviors that might hinder your progress, making it easier for you to accomplish IT.

When it comes to e-mail, all of us have received this dreaded auto reply: "I am out of the office and will not return until . . ." "I will have limited access to e-mail and will respond when I return." When checking responses to a recent e-newsletter we sent, we came across this quite unique auto reply: "Thank you for your message. Due to some upcoming deadlines and my current workload, I will be checking e-mail only a couple of times each day. If you need immediate assistance, please call . . ." Now, there's a person who knows the value of communicating IT. People e-mailing her now know that she will not respond as quickly as she typically does because she's choosing to make e-mail a lesser priority. Why? Because she's working on IT.

For managers and leaders, this need to communicate IT takes on even greater significance. It announces to the person's team where her energy will be focused—and possibly their energy as well. Communicating a simple and clearly defined goal creates awareness and captures the imagination of the people around you.

Communicating your values, goals, and activities creates a framework of support that helps you in your quest to achieve what is most important to you.

Communicating a simple
and clearly defined goal
creates awareness and
captures the imagination
of the people around you.

During preparation for the first Apollo mission to space, a custodian cleaning the restrooms at NASA was asked about her job responsibilities. Her reply? "I'm working to put a man on the moon." She knew that her work was playing a part in achieving NASA's overall goal of accomplishing IT, the same as a rocket scientist's.

TO REVEAL YOUR PASSION AND VISION (THE HEART OF IT)

When communicating to others about IT, don't just give them a heap of facts, figures, whys, and why-nots. Include the heart behind what you're doing. Your numbers and research will go a long way in explaining why you have chosen IT, but your ability to communicate your vision and passion is what will convince them of ITS importance and your level of commitment.

And don't just communicate the benefits IT has for you; share why IT should be important to them as well. Include the benefits to their family or organization. Especially for challenging projects, people want to see that you genuinely believe there's reason behind your madness and light at the end of the tunnel. When you share the heart and significance underlying IT, your family and associates also will share the sense of urgency behind the action. Whether you're solving a problem or seizing an opportunity, the urgency and passion that you project will cause people to either board your train or get out of the way.

SO OTHERS KNOW CHANGE IS COMING

If all ITS were pleasant undertakings, you might not be reading this book. There will often be some difficult times ahead for both you and others in your journey to accomplish IT. We'll focus later on how to work on IT with others, but for now it's important to remember that communicating IT warns others that things will change not only for you but for them as well. As you plan your communication, ask yourself these questions:

- What's in IT for them?
- Why should they be excited about IT for me?
- Why should they be excited about IT for themselves?

You might not want to assume that they'll perceive the value of IT as you do—especially if IT will require a wrenching change in attitude or behavior on their part. In fact, the greater the change needed to accomplish IT, the more critical it is that everyone buys in to the vision underlying the change. A small-business owner might announce, "We've postponed hiring a new person to replace Jim until our revenue is more stable. We'll be shorthanded for a while, but it's better than staffing up now and facing the need for layoffs if the market doesn't turn around." For a family, cutting back on expenses might be IT, so everyone needs to visualize the ultimate outcome of making uncomfortable changes. Focusing on the goal—paying off the credit card balance or being able to afford a new car—as an incentive, individual family members will be more willing to look for ways to conserve or to set aside their desires for immediate gratification.

The Benefits of Communicating It to Others

Here are some examples of the benefits of communicating IT to others.

CREATING A SHARED BUCKET FOR INFORMATION

As people go about their daily activities, they'll come across ideas and information that remind them of you and your IT. If they really understand your vision and the passion underlying IT, they'll most likely share what they come across.

Jones has a file folder of old newspaper and magazine articles his mom and dad collected for him once they knew he dreamed of becoming a professional speaker. Some are advice columns from people like Dear Abby. Other articles include excerpts from graduation speeches given at local colleges or stories about leadership or service. Still others highlight the lives of successful people in his area like Nido Qubein, professional speaker, author, and president of High Point University. In the days before the Internet, he would refer to the folder often when needing a story, illustration, or even a humorous anecdote. He would never have had this resource if he had kept his dream to himself.

If you think about it, one of the real values of social networking is that you can very efficiently tell a lot of people about your IT and invite their ideas and feedback. Have you ever posted on a social media site that you're going to travel to a particular place and would like suggestions on what to do while you're there? The wealth of information that's likely to pour in from your Facebook friends might amaze you. People are eager to share their experiences and knowledge if you give them an opportunity.

REFINING IT . . . OR DISCOVERING YOU SHOULD THROW IT BACK INTO THE FUNNEL

You might think you've used all of the correct filters to zero in on IT, but when you reveal IT to a group, they might well have different perspectives. Their disagreement probably won't be with your core morals, beliefs, goals, or mission filters; instead, they're likely to raise practical considerations—issues such as, Is this the right time? or Where are we going to get the resources? or Who has the time to take the lead on such an undertaking? Discussing the appropriateness of IT can often benefit from an exchange of uncertainties and reassurances. Being questioned or challenged will also test whether you indeed have the passion and heart to make IT a reality. Other people's questions might bring to light oversights in your plan for accomplishing IT, and how IT could impact things beyond your limited view. With luck, the feedback gained in these discussions will help expedite the completion of IT, so you and the others affected can efficiently move on toward the next opportunity.

If, after discussion, you find that your IT isn't the ideal IT after all, you might consider using the Three-D strategy: *delegate IT* (move it to someone else's funnel), *delete IT* (toss it out of the funnel entirely), or *delay IT* (wait until circumstances are more conducive to IT being embraced by those around you and/or the timing for getting IT accomplished is better).

ESTABLISHING ACCOUNTABILITY

You might need to accept accountability and tolerate some pressure once you've announced your goal to others, especially if there's a deadline involved. You might encounter coworkers asking you how IT's going whenever they pass you in the hallway. Most will be asking out of genuine interest and will be sincerely eager to

see you succeed (as we'll discuss in a moment). But
some might be reminding you that you've made prom-
ises and that the clock is ticking.

Consider Joe. He decides to communicate to his wife
his goal of losing fifteen pounds before his birthday. A
few weeks later, he's piling the potatoes on his plate
at dinner. A simple glance, an "innocent" question
from his wife—"How's that new diet working out for
you?"—may be all it takes to shame him into shoveling
half of those spuds back into the bowl.

You might see the attention of others as pressure,
but bear in mind there are two kinds of stress: *eustress* (positive) and *distress* (negative). Whether that
pressure comes from within yourself—I promised I'd
have this ready by Monday morning, so I'd better plan
on staying up late—or you're aware of people moni-
toring whether you're going to make your goal, you
have the option of viewing whatever stress you encounter as eustress, pressure that drives you forward
to your goal.

Look at the retail industry and its desire for in-
creased levels of customer feedback. From the cashier
asking "Did you find everything okay?" to the satisfaction surveys attached to your receipt to the online requests that pop up requesting that you evaluate your
shopping or customer-support experience, feedback
is a valuable asset to an organization that serves the
public. By communicating this IT to their customers,

retailers are saying, "Help us improve by holding us accountable."

Awareness of the need for accountability is particularly sharp if you're asking people around you to make sacrifices to help you accomplish IT. A coworker takes on some of your responsibilities for a few days while you finish up a major project . . . Employees in a small business work extra hours during the holiday season to make sure every customer is served . . . Your family tolerates your absence at the dinner table while you're putting the finishing touches on a new idea . . . You'd be surprised how many people willingly make sacrifices if they care about you and respect you and your goals.

But be very careful of communicating IT to others and then failing to follow through. Your failure to work toward your stated goal after you've solicited sacrifices from others might jeopardize their willingness to help you in the future. The next time their response might be, Why bother?

Also, be mindful of sharing the credit with others once the goal has been achieved. Sharing the credit, even if the project has been your IT and you did most of the work, is an incentive for others to work with you in the future. An "attitude of gratitude" goes a long way in making those who helped you out feel respected and appreciated—and therefore predisposed to pitch in again the next time you ask.

REMOVING THE VACUUM OF SUSPICION AND
CONFUSION

Have you ever heard someone say, "If people don't
know the truth, they'll invent it"? Meghan is the HR
director at a small hospital. Imagine that her IT for
one week is to spend one uninterrupted hour in her
office each day: door closed, phone switched to voice
mail, and no immediate replies to e-mails. Meghan
doesn't tell anyone about her commitment to herself
to establish this positive new routine; she assumes
it's too personal and trivial to be any of their concern.
A few days later, however, a coworker tries to find
Meghan during her no-interruptions hour, but she's
nowhere to be found. He walks away, asking others
where Meghan has gone off to, but no one knows. Is
something wrong? She was seen in the morning as
she arrived for work. Another coworker says, "I've
noticed that her door has been closed a lot," and the
search for Meghan begins to take on an ominous tone.
By noon, Meghan's rumored to have a terminal disease, to be coping with marital problems, and to be
looking for a new job. Office paranoia? Of course! But
unjustified? Not really.

When IT is a mystery, it's human nature for people to
come up with their own explanations. It's also human
nature for the most absurd rumors to have the most
persistence. Rather than believing a harmless, simple

explanation, people tend to prefer the most sensational and damaging, if least plausible, explanation.

When those around you are not aware of your IT, you may find they're suspicious and defensive rather than supportive. An information vacuum can not only slow progress, it can effectively derail IT.

Even worse is a "white lie" or an attempt to "spin" known facts in an attempt to give progress on IT a better appearance than it deserves.

We were at a professional development conference with about ten thousand attendees. The conference made a big deal about "going green" that year and chose not to print the customary program catalog to conserve paper. Sounds noble enough. Strangely, however, the organizers still saw fit to serve ten thousand lunches per day in large, printed cardboard boxes when they could have chosen any number of green alternatives. The word soon spread that the organizers' real IT behind not printing the program catalog was simply to save money, at the inconvenience of paying attendees. The organization's stated goal to go green in one area was undermined by this oversight in another area.

STIRRING THE **IT** THAT LIES WITHIN OTHERS

When we received confirmation that our first book, *Juggling Elephants*, was going to be published, a strange thing happened in many conversations about

*When those around you
are not aware of IT or your
activities associated with
IT, you may find that they
are suspicious and less
than supportive.*

our new IT: friends and business associates alike told us they had always wanted to write a book. In some cases, they had chapters or whole books already written, but they had let their enthusiasm go cold—that is, until our sharing of our IT brought their own ITS to the surface again.

Hearing about someone's success can often spark a fire in others and provide the much-needed confidence to go for IT. Some of the best inspirational or motivational speakers are those who have a personal story: "I faced defeat, injury, birth defects, setbacks, walking to school in snow uphill both ways . . . yet I accomplished IT. So can you!" As Albert Schweitzer once said, "Example is not the main thing influencing others. It is the only thing."

We frequently come in contact with people who've overcome monumental obstacles to achieve success: cancer survivors, single parents, and even some small-business owners make up the short list. We always come away from conversations with such people searching our own funnels more intensely, looking for possibilities that will really make a difference in this world. Your willingness to share your own story about achieving IT against daunting odds can inspire others to exceptional performance and encourage them to have confidence that their own unique IT is achievable.

Your willingness to share your own story about achieving IT, despite daunting odds, can encourage others to have confidence that their own IT is achievable.

BRINGING OTHERS ON BOARD WITH YOU AND YOUR ITS

Most people want to align themselves with others who are confident about where they are going. We frequently see this when speaking to corporate groups. Prior to our remarks at a conference or company meeting, a high-ranking individual in the organization often will introduce or roll out a new IT. It's interesting to observe the audience at this point. Leaders who are known to have the trust of the group because they regularly fulfill their commitment to their ITS get a positive response. But those who are constantly changing IT based on the "flavor of the month" and with little or no follow-through are clearly regarded as being full of "it"—the other kind.

During the Gulf of Mexico oil spill of 2010, BP CEO Tony Hayward gave all of us a demonstration of how to indicate to the world you are not full of the right kind of IT. In an interview at the peak of the crisis, in a moment of frustration, he described the stress of leadership by saying, "I want my life back." This comment didn't go over very well, as those whose livelihoods were devastated by the spill reacted with "Well, we do, too!" Hayward lost the public's confidence that BP was serious about the IT of the moment: getting the leak plugged and returning the gulf to normal.

What a difference a few careful words could have made! When Hayward said, "I want my life back," he could have added, " . . . but I won't get it back until we've helped every person affected by this spill regain what they've lost." As you probably already know, he was fired a short time later.

A Communication Checkup

Let's revisit the beginning of the chapter, where we imagined interviewing those who are closest to you to test whether or not you've successfully communicated your IT. You might be confident you would pass the test with flying colors. Why not actually test it for yourself?

An eye-opening exercise is to do your own interviewing. Ask friends, family, colleagues, customers, vendors, and even casual acquaintances what they think is your IT. Any surprises? Sometimes your actions speak louder than your stated intentions. Hearing how others would describe your IT can tell you the following:

- How well am I communicating IT?
- How well do I walk the talk; how well do my actions align with my commitment?
- Are the ITS that other people attribute to me actually in my funnel and in line with my filters?

From a professional standpoint, you might find that you're on a completely different page from your boss and that you're focusing on the wrong areas.

It's Time to Ride

Paul Revere's name is familiar to most Americans who remember their elementary school lessons. His horseback ride through the New England countryside is legendary. His brave journey alerting the colonists of the British invasion helped ensure that England would not extinguish the colonists' burning desire for freedom in the 1770s. He definitely was a man who knew the value of communicating IT.

Most of us who know of Paul Revere's ride overlook the fact that there was another rider who set out that night with the same IT in mind. His name was William Dawes. In his book *The Tipping Point*, Malcolm Gladwell tells us more about this significant, if less familiar, figure in history. He writes, "His ride yielded little more than a few men from one small community showing up to meet the British army."

The difference? Paul Revere knew when, how, and to whom to communicate IT. He had visited the towns and villages, had talked with their citizens, and had stirred a vision within them. When the British finally were coming, everything was in place—making IT all about execution.

If you have shared IT with those around you with all of the passion, purpose, and clarity you could muster, then it might be time to call an architect to create the plans. Your vacant lot is ready for a makeover.

Chapter 5

_____

Planning for I<small>T</small>

ITS RARELY SCREAM AT US. THEY WAIT

PATIENTLY BEHIND EVERYTHING ELSE.

Completing a few well-planned ITS brings more success
and satisfaction than completing a whole long list of everything else.

Identifying the Important Thing you could be doing and then creating the environment to accomplish IT
can be the easy part. Lots of people discover their IT or
at least have a sense for what IT should be . . . but stop
there.

Think of inaction as if it were a new car sitting in
your driveway, gassed up and ready to go, but never
actually going anywhere because you never get around
to opening the door and driving it. Inaction is also like
deciding you're going to get into shape through diet
and exercise. You buy books on nutrition and purchase

a gym membership, but then you never read the books and formulate a plan, you don't go to the gym, or you fail to pass up a chance to indulge in fattening food.

Individuals and organizations often develop elaborate plans to improve their attitudes, income, and prospects for future performance, but then they fail to follow through on the plan. What determines success or failure is both a plan and the execution of that plan. Once you've sorted through all your options and pinpointed IT, the next question you'll need to ask yourself is, How can I make sure I successfully accomplish IT? This chapter outlines a process not only for building a plan but also for making certain that plan is carried out.

Build the Plan for It

Begin, like a battlefield commander or an architect, by surveying the landscape.

Going back to the concept of your vacant lot, consider that there are, inevitably, established realities that you can neither ignore nor remove—a tree you want to preserve, a boulder that can't be dug out and hauled off, the zoning restrictions in place to prevent property owners from installing sawmills in residential developments or strip clubs next to schoolyards. You rarely work on ITs divorced from everything else in the world.

As you plan to accomplish IT, consider other items that are already in place for the year, month, or general time frame involved in your journey.

As you plan to accomplish IT, consider other priorities already on your schedule for the year, month, or week ahead. They could include everything from conferences you're obligated to attend to limited staffing that can't be ramped up overnight. In your personal life, birthdays, anniversaries, weddings, soccer schedules, and PTA meetings are already part of your calendar and can't be pushed aside. The big question to answer is: How do I accomplish IT given the commitments I already have in place?

As you think ahead to taking action on IT next week, next month, or next year, consider the obstacles and limitations likely to impede your progress. Make a list! It may be finances: How are you going to pay for IT? Education: Do you have the necessary skills and knowledge? If not, how will you gain them and how long will that take? Personnel: Do you have the right people in place and do they share your commitment? For whatever roadblocks and speed bumps you can anticipate, prepare work-arounds and alternate routes.

One great example of planning and executing a complex project was in the L.A. news—the transport of a 340-ton boulder from Riverside, California, to the Los Angeles County Museum of Art, where it would be part of a permanent installation by a conceptual artist. It required engineering of a huge, unique vehicle, closing off streets and clearing parked cars, constructing special cranes, and inching this boulder along at baby-step speed. What's most appealing about the story is that the artist conceived of this impossible thing, an abstract statement, and then heaven and earth had to be moved to make it a reality. And it came out precisely the way he imagined it.

IDENTIFY GENERAL STEPS TO ACCOMPLISH IT

If the IT you are working on is large or complex, focus on the more general steps to accomplishing IT; the details can come later.

For example, if IT for you is earning your MBA or some higher degree or certification, at the outset you might focus on how you will secure tuition and which school you want to attend. Choosing the actual courses you'll be taking or planning your daily routine can come later. Determine five to seven milestones on the way to accomplishing IT, and map out in general terms how you'll move from one to the next.

DETERMINE MILESTONES

Simply put: What do you want to accomplish, and by when? People identify their IT but then let time pass until IT is no longer relevant. Here are two suggestions to keep in mind when setting milestones on the way toward completing IT:

- Set a deadline. Pick a date for completion and then plan backward, determining as realistically as possible how much time will be allocated for each step along the trajectory to reaching that deadline. If the time required by all the steps added together extends well beyond your deadline, ask yourself whether it's possible for several subprojects to proceed in parallel, or put your imagination to work coming up with unconventional but workable shortcuts.
- Equip yourself with ways to measure work in progress. Your planning might indicate you'll reach your goal with plenty of time to spare, but real-world situations often prove to be stubbornly unyielding—as engineers say, "In theory, theory and practice are identical. In practice, they're not." If you set daily or weekly benchmarks and then have a system to compare actual progress against predetermined interim goals, you'll at least avoid being surprised too late to make adjustments.

BREAK **IT** DOWN INTO SMALL STEPS

There's an old riddle that asks, "How do you eat an elephant?" The solution? "One bite at a time." Instead of focusing on the end result far off over the horizon and feeling overwhelmed, ask yourself what you could do in the next moment to move toward IT. Simply writing down interim goals and realizing that each is eminently doable might be just the confidence builder needed to launch you off the starting block.

Our friend Ronnie is a "power-pole runner." No, he doesn't work on utility lines—he participates in running events. When Ronnie sets a daunting distance to run in his daily training, he doesn't think about the total distance. Rather, he tells himself as he's running that he just needs to make it to the next power pole. He pushes his endurance pole by pole until he finds, almost as a side effect, that he's able to go the full distance.

Think about how much you could accomplish by working toward IT for just fifteen or thirty minutes each day. At an average of just thirty minutes per day, that's 150 minutes each week (giving yourself two days off), approximately ten hours per month, and 120 hours per year—that's three weeks of full-time labor! Even though you may never be able to set aside all those hours as one block of time, you can tackle a daunting IT by consistently nibbling away at it each day to get it done.

Create Your Actual Plan for IT

Now that you've surveyed the landscape where you'll be staging IT and mentally prepared yourself for the long haul, it's time to roll up your sleeves and lay out your schedule. Realistic planning is key. Reserve for yourself regularly scheduled uninterrupted time isolated from whatever else is going on in your life, and visualize what you'll accomplish by the end of each session. Review your to-do list, the events on your schedule you can't blow off or wouldn't miss for the world—visiting that new supplier's factory in China, attending your daughter's debut in the role of Goldilocks—and think of every other moment on your calendar as time available for ɪᴛ. Dedicate yourself to keeping those vague-agenda office meetings, impulsive volunteer commitments, and meandering weekend backyard projects from spreading like kudzu into the rest of your calendar, and you'll find you have all the time you need for ɪᴛ. Remember, ɪᴛ is the Important Thing—don't feel guilty about making everything else take a number and wait its turn.

When you choose to plan is up to you. For some, the best time for lining up a day's activities is first thing in the morning. For others, the end of the day is ideal for reviewing today's accomplishments and setting tomorrow's goals. Whichever you choose, commit to making a solid plan for each and every day, if you want your ɪᴛ to be more than just a "someday when I have time" kind of dream.

Consider these time-tested tips when planning your stepping-stones toward ɪᴛ:

- Write things down. This tip is as old as the invention of hieroglyphics, but we all know its value. Getting

Think about what you could do working on some element of IT for just fifteen to thirty minutes a day.

things out of your head and onto paper (or into a computer file or smartphone app) frees your memory for moment-to-moment tasks. And if something's in ink on paper (or pixels on a screen), you can't tell yourself it slipped your mind.

- Plan to focus on the ITS that require a lot of mental work at the beginning of the day, when you're fresh and energetic. Your energy level and ability to focus on brain-straining ITS decrease as the day goes on. Plan for demanding mental labor early and physical tasks later when your muscles need a workout and your brain needs to recharge.

- Prioritize, prioritize, prioritize. The number of potential tasks you could choose to work on at any given moment is infinite. Prioritizing allows you to devote your brainpower to getting one thing done rather than endlessly bouncing from possibility to possibility.

- Do a double-check on your to-do list. Once you have your prioritized to-do list, correlate it with a list of the hours in the day. (You can use a purchased daily planner, the calendar in Outlook, or simply a sheet of paper.) Starting with your highest-priority task, block out when you are going to begin it and how long it will take. Continue down your task list, blocking out times for each task. Don't be upset if you run out of hours in the day about halfway through your list—that's okay, as long as you've genuinely made IT the top priority on your schedule. "Desirable but not crucial" tasks can be scheduled to tomorrow or another day. Forgive yourself for not accomplishing everything you wanted to do—you're human, after all—but respect yourself for tending to the Important Thing.

- Employ the Four-D strategy. We've already discussed the Three D's—delegate, delete, or delay—but it's worth remembering one more D: *do!* More often than we admit, tasks that ought to take only a couple of minutes to complete end up taking much more time when they've been put off. In many cases, the most effective way of keeping a molehill from becoming a mountain is simply to finish it while it's manageable. A good example might be that science fair project on electricity you promised to help your son with. If you had given him a few pointers weeks before the project was due, your son might have had just enough of a leg up to research it and confidently assemble it himself. But since you've told him, "Not tonight, tomorrow for sure," right up until the day before his presentation is due, your sense of having let him down drives you to stay up half the night building most of his project for him and trying to teach him everything you know about electrical engineering.
- Create gaps and buffers of time. Be realistic about what you can accomplish in an hour or in a day.

Allow time for the inevitable interruptions and crises. If your schedule is too full, the tendency is to drop the Important Things for the merely urgent ones. Research suggests that tasks typically take 20 percent more time than expected. So if you have a task you think will take an hour, add another twelve or fifteen minutes just in case. This allows you to accomplish it yet still get to the other ITS that are not so patiently waiting their turn.

- Develop a habit or build a routine into your plan. A routine can walk you through a series of ITS that need to be accomplished on a regular basis. These items don't usually require the same level of concentration or planning as a major IT, but they can be just as time- and energy-consuming if you let them. If you give some thought to how best to order tasks, the most logical and productive flow, you can execute a series of tasks almost as if it's a single task. Then combining a routine with other routines in the right order can multiply that effect, allowing you to efficiently, effectively, and easily accomplish much more than if you grapple with each task independently.

     For example, you might have a morning work routine—plan the day, check e-mail, check voice mail, review information for meetings, then meet with someone on your team. You probably find that when you're able to follow the entire routine as a block, without interruption, your day is effective and organized. But if the full routine doesn't happen, you're likely to feel scattered and reactive, like you're playing "catch-up" all day.

While looking for items to package into routines or habits, watch out for routines that don't help you accomplish IT, too. For example, you might come home from work, eat dinner, do the dishes, sit down, turn on the TV, and then channel surf the rest of the evening. You might realize this routine puts a "period" to the end of your day, and that by habitually following this routine, you're stifling your instinct to focus on anything of greater importance. Define and develop positive routines; remove negative routines from your schedule.

In his book *What It Takes to Be #1*, Vince Lombardi wrote, "Habits are those actions that get us through our day without a whole lot of conscious thought on our part. It's our habits, those actions that flow from our thoughts, beliefs, and words, that distinguish winners from everyone else."

Constantly seeking the most important possibility (and accomplishing the resulting IT) fosters desirable behaviors such as focus, goal setting, planning, organizing, and evaluating. Engage in these behaviors long enough, and they become second nature.

Keep track of time while you work on IT. To ensure

that you focus on IT for a predetermined period of time, set the alarm on your mobile phone or wristwatch, or buy a small timer that you can set for the length of time you've dedicated to focusing on your task. When the alarm rings, feel free to move on to the next IT— and don't be surprised if you're not ready to. Schedule in some time after your alarm rings to wrap up what you're working on before you must begin your next activity. If you're reluctant to move on because you're making such fantastic progress with IT, consider how your schedule will have to be rearranged and what won't get done as a result of sticking with that particular IT.

Plan with Family Members

Your plan to work on IT could quickly be in danger if you neglect to take the schedules of others into account. For your family, consider setting up a central family-coordination calendar with the rule that if something doesn't get on the calendar, it doesn't happen—period. It doesn't have to be hung on the kitchen wall; with today's technology (including applications like Google Calendar and Outlook's Calendar), everyone can have access to a shared calendar from wherever they are. Also, sit down as a family at or before the beginning of the week for a planning session. What activities are going on in the next few days or weeks? Who needs a ride somewhere, and when? Can we schedule time to actually sit down and eat a meal together? What about time for a vacation when everyone is free? Sessions like this can be vital in a household with teenagers. A weekly planning meeting doesn't take much time and acts as "an ounce of prevention" for the week. Family-relationship planning not only will help you get a standing ovation when that vacation finally comes, but it also will help you in your job. When you have a busy schedule at work, the last thing you need is to be distracted with shuttling your twelve-year-old to the swim meet she forgot to tell you about, or worrying about the great mystery of why your sixteen-year-old desperately went "out" (somewhere) to "hang" (whatever that means). Family and relationship planning allows you to stay focused, confident it's safe to keep working on a "work IT," though you'd drop everything to deal with an IT involving those you love and feel responsible for.

Plan with Your Team Members at Work

Just as planning with your family is important, so, too, is planning with your team at work. You might find that meeting on Fridays to review the events of the past week and plan for the next is effective. Or you might find that meeting first thing Monday is more productive for your team. Either way, dedicate some time to going over things such as approaching dead-

A weekly planning meeting doesn't take much time and acts as "an ounce of prevention" for the week.

lines, project updates, next steps, upcoming events, important meetings, adjustments to expectations, and unexpected developments that call for additional resources to move things forward. We expand on this idea in chapter 9, Working with Others on I<small>T</small>.

A Plan Improves Spontaneity or Creativity Around I<small>*T*</small>

When we speak to a group, we often ask, "How many of you sit down and formally plan your day?" We typically get only a few hands—maybe 10 percent of the audience. When we ask for reasons why attendees don't plan their day, the first answer almost always is "I don't have time." The second most common answer is "Planning my day is too confining and doesn't allow me to be spontaneous or deal with the 'brush fires' that come up."

The reality is that spontaneity needs to be coupled with training, planning, and preparation to be effective. You can't draw from a dry well. That's why those in some lines of work (firefighters, professional athletes, and those in the military) constantly run drills to prepare for when the unexpected occurs.

It's the job of firefighters and other first responders to deal with emergencies, and each emergency is unique. No one plans to have an emergency. Firefighters continually train and rehearse possible courses of action so that when a unique, challenging situation arises, they can react as if it's something they've dealt with successfully a hundred times already. Each call for help is unique, but the procedures and best practices they've rehearsed are executed to the letter; spontaneity and creative on-the-spot problem solving seldom enter into it—otherwise, mistakes are made and lives are lost. When firefighters arrive on a scene, they immediately start working through a mental checklist, an established decision tree known to determine the best actions, given the many variables, to keep them successful and safe.

Lives might not be on the line in your job—you might even get paid for being creative and spontaneous—but if you're flying from one activity to another, making up your plan as you go along, mistakes will be made and opportunities lost. You certainly can fill your day with activity and get a lot accomplished when you work without a plan, but the real question is: Did you work on it?

Consider another benefit of planning as you strive for spontaneity and deal with emergencies or interruptions: You started your day by sitting down and planning it out. You have just started on the most important of all the options fanned out before you for the day when the phone rings and you have an unexpected issue to deal with. So much for your plan, right? Wrong! You'll still return to your desk once the fire is out, and if you have planned and prioritized what's

A plan improves spontaneity or creativity around IT.

most important, you'll quickly pick up where you left off. Otherwise, you'll have to spend additional time asking yourself, Now, what was I doing? or debating whether you should just skip that most Important Thing for now and work on something trivial instead. You'll no doubt have less time to accomplish your plan, but if you've properly used your filters, you can immediately, confidently refocus on your IT.

Create Urgency Around It

The beginning of a new year is always touted as a good time for changing behaviors because it's naturally regarded as a clean slate. You might choose to create your plan at the end of your organization's fiscal year—or just after you've completed an intense project and are feeling a positive sense of accomplishment. Or maybe it's a birthday, anniversary, or some other significant milestone. The key is that the moment offers you a sense that "now's the time." Having the mental energy and clarity of thought to create the best plan is essential. Trying to formulate a complex new plan in moments of frustration, when you're overwhelmed or habituated to a process you've been involved in for months, may lead to failure. The odds for success are better if you feel you have had a moment to catch your breath and are starting fresh.

"Someday," "one day," and "when the time is right"

don't encourage much momentum. In fact, they can remove almost every ounce of accountability and urgency from a plan to accomplish anything. In your journey to accomplish IT, consider establishing firm starting dates and milestones for every part of your plan. To encourage yourself to set firm deadlines to accomplish IT, and to create a sense of urgency, ask yourself two questions:

1. WHAT WILL I LOSE (OR CONTINUE TO LOSE) IF I DON'T ACCOMPLISH IT?

Be specific, and factor in long-term loss. Many of us engage in hyperbolic discounting—the human tendency to prefer smaller payoffs now over larger payoffs later. Such thinking leads us to essentially disregard the future when it requires sacrifices in the present.

America's Big Three automakers provide a strong example of organizations that engaged in hyperbolic discounting. While fuel prices and consumer demand were changing in the early 2000s, automakers continued to produce the same types of vehicles they had made when gas was relatively cheap and huge vehicles were the coolest new thing. They acted as if the future wasn't coming . . . or was of little importance. Why? They valued the smaller payoff of low retooling and development costs (and therefore higher shareholder returns) in that moment more than the potential bigger payoff of being ready with new products that suited a changed market in the future.

Their discounting had drastic consequences that could have been avoided if they had placed more emphasis on the future. What's your cost tomorrow for not working on IT today?

Let's look at the potential loss another way: Imagine that Stan has an employee named Scott. Stan knows his IT is to talk with Scott about his poor job performance, but he just can't bring himself to have the conversation. What is he losing? At first glance, Stan might think it's just a few moments of frustration every day or two. If Stan takes a closer look, however, he might see that he's losing the productivity of two employees: Scott and himself. In addition, Stan is missing out on any opportunity to improve the situation (either Scott changes or he's gone). And what about the other five employees in the department who are aware of the situation? Think they can't see what's going on? Now Stan is losing productivity from seven people, and possibly their respect, for not handling the situation as expeditiously as he could. The conversation might just take on greater urgency if Stan viewed it from that perspective.

2. WHO WILL SUFFER IF I DON'T ACCOMPLISH IT?

Jan is a graphic design specialist for a retail clothing company. Let's say her IT is to be more actively engaged with her family after work—her relationships are at the breaking point. Unfortunately, she continues bringing work home, and nights and weekends are often filled with quick, furtive bursts of reviewing e-mails or tweaking designs. She tries to rationalize by saying to herself, "At least I'm home," but she knows that's a cop-out. Her children can tell when her focus is somewhere else. Jan's spouse isn't immune, either. He, too, can tell when her mind is somewhere else; in fact, Jan's husband finds that he unconsciously limits conversation with her because of her constant obsession with her smartphone that takes her attention away from him.

If you honestly reflect on why it isn't getting accomplished in your own life, you can probably trace it back to saying yes to too many projects at work or not setting boundaries between work and life. At the time you say yes, you think it will affect only you, but your experience tells you you're just wearing blinders that limit your perception of the wider issue.

From an organizational level, what does your company stand to lose if you're not focused on it? Opportunity? Market share? Revenue? If you manage other people, the loss grows exponentially and very quickly.

Build Incentives and Rewards into the Plan for IT

In one *Calvin and Hobbes* cartoon strip, the six-year-old Calvin is persuaded by his dad to eat his broccoli. When he asks, "Why?" his dad replies, "It will build your character."

If you were Calvin, would you jump right in and devour those smelly florets? Almost from birth we're wired to expect tangible rewards for doing something right, well, or quickly. As we get older, we usually become more intrinsically motivated—virtue is its own reward—but we're still more willing to move outside our comfort space if we expect to receive some benefit (even if it's just self-satisfaction).

When Todd consults with sales managers on creating a sales strategy, he often asks questions such as, What's your incentive to sell this product or service? What's your incentive to make outbound calls every day? or Does your compensation or incentive program drive the behaviors that you're looking for or that will bring success [that is, sales]? When working with organizations that are having trouble getting people on board with change, some of the most clarifying questions are: What's their incentive to change? and What's in IT for them?

Also consider what's in IT for you personally if you change your ways. It's easy to stay busy working on stuff or just filling time. With a busy schedule and sometimes very little support from others, creating a plan to accomplish IT can be a daunting task.

One way you can stay on course is to bribe yourself into working on IT.

Todd has a friend with a rather unusual method for keeping himself working on his ITS, even when he doesn't feel like it. He currently juggles a career as a physician and a family that includes his spouse and three young children. He shared with us some great insights and ideas about motivation and sticking to a "healthy self-improvement routine"—even when that isn't easy. With his permission, here are some of his thoughts we found helpful:

> I exercise three to four times per week in the winter, five to seven times per week in the summer, mostly cycling (more spinning in winter). I know that I must exercise regularly in order to have the energy and endurance for the rest of my life's activities. Ironically, although I love to ride and I do it often, I almost never feel like riding. I consistently work nine- to twelve-hour days (or nights), so when I get home, I'm beat. I feel spent, although rationally I know that I'm more mentally drained than physically weary. Either way, I honestly don't feel like jumping on the bike to exercise—but I know that exercising

regularly means you have to do it even when you don't feel like it. Just like having a job means going to work even when you don't feel like it.

By far, the path of least resistance is to grab a snack and hit the sofa. My mind and body are telling me that I'm too spent to exercise, but deep down, as I know from experience, that probably isn't true. So I have to trick myself into getting on the bike instead of getting on the couch (or plopping down in front of the computer). I tell myself that I'll just ride to the mouth of the canyon, a short six minutes from my house. I tell myself that if I still feel lousy when I get there, I'll turn around and come home to the couch, guilt-free. This gets me over that important first hurdle: changing into my cycling clothes, mixing a bottle of Gatorade, getting out on the bike, turning the cranks in the fresh air.

I'm sincere in my promise to turn around if I still feel poorly at the mouth of the canyon, but I've done so less than a half-dozen times in more than ten years—the rare occasions when the "test" proved that I really was too exhausted or too ill to ride. The overwhelming majority of times, I feel a little bit better by the time I get to the mouth of the canyon. Then I tell myself, "Just up to the Cutler Trailhead [about one third of the way up the canyon], and if I'm not really into it by then, I'll allow myself to turn back."

Again, I've turned back at the trailhead only a half dozen or so times. I nearly always feel quite a bit better (or at least no worse) by the time I get there. I still might not be in the mood to keep going, so, if necessary, I make myself another deal . . . and so on. More often than not, by the time I hit the trailhead, I've forgotten all about feeling poorly, and my mind has moved on to better things. I'm able to clear my head and do some of my best thinking on the bike. Before I know it, I'm summiting the canyon, feeling mentally and physically refreshed. With the day's stress left behind and my thoughts newly focused, I can continue the ride until I return home, energized to do something productive rather than resigned to vegetate for the rest of the evening.

It's funny . . . I've "tricked" myself literally thousands of times this way over the years, but it's never lost its effectiveness. By breaking an intimidatingly long ride down into manageable bites, I'm able to get through a great workout that I'd have otherwise skipped. While some people would say, "I don't have time and energy to exercise—I've got work to do," I know that I simply can't afford the waste of not refocusing and reenergizing through exercise.

Create Initial Momentum to Accomplish IT

Remember the Law of Inertia? It states that an object at rest tends to stay at rest until an outside force is applied to it—in other words, the vacant lot tends to stay vacant. The most difficult part is to start the motion. We'll talk more about "doing IT" in the next chapter, but, for now, consider these ideas for getting your IT into gear:

- Contact someone to celebrate with you when you tell him about your plans. Talking with someone else also creates accountability.
- Physically capture what you know about what's required to accomplish IT. Record your thoughts on your phone, call your voice mail and leave a message, send yourself an e-mail, or use old-fashioned pen and paper—the actual method doesn't matter. What does matter is that you're replacing time and mental energy taken up by inaction, fear, or insecurity (whatever reason IT wasn't accomplished before) with thoughts and plans for how to get IT done. Not every step in your journey to accomplish IT will require mortgaging your home, quitting your job, or speaking in front of a thousand people. Seeing and then achieving the smaller elements of the equation helps build much-needed momentum.

Build Action on It into Every Moment

As you become more fully aware of the value of always executing your plan for IT, you may find yourself going through each day asking these questions:

- What is IT for me?
- Why do I believe in IT?
- How do I get to IT?
- How do I do IT?

Granted, you'll be working on more than one IT in a day, a week, a month, and certainly in a lifetime, but you can work on only one IT at a time. If you create a plan to accomplish each IT, your days have the potential to go much more smoothly—and you're more likely to get your most Important Things done. You'll know where your time and energy need to be applied.

You're setting yourself up to achieve more success at work, grow your relationships, and become more of the person you want to be. Even one minute of your life spent not focusing on IT creates the chance that some opportunity could forever be lost to the rush of chasing "everything else."

You know where your time and energy need to be spent.

I have only just a minute, only sixty seconds in it.
Forced upon me, can't refuse it.
Didn't seek it, didn't choose it.
But it's up to me to use it.
I must suffer if I lose it.
Give account if I abuse it.
Just a tiny little minute, but eternity is in it.

—ANONYMOUS

Chapter 6

Doing I*T*

FAILURE AT AN **IT** IS OFTEN BETTER THAN
SUCCESS AT SOMETHING ELSE.

A seemingly small number of people have the capacity to get everything done. They're on top of deadlines, prepared when called upon, and can execute well at a moment's notice. It would appear as if their funnel doesn't narrow at the bottom—everything imaginable flows through to completion. They have an amazing ability to make things happen.

You can be such a person.

Conversely, many people have a very narrow outlet at the bottom of their funnel. They may have all sorts of plans, possibilities, and ideas but fall short when it comes to executing them . . . they simply can't get IT done.

You can be that person as well.

This chapter is all about the key strategies the first group of individuals follow—what makes them so successful and what they do or don't do that results in their ability to get IT done. As you read this chapter, ask yourself, Which of these strategies are crucial for me to get my particular IT done?

Focus on It

Harry Emerson Fosdick, a famous clergyman in the early twentieth century, once said, "No horse gets anywhere until he is harnessed. No steam or gas ever drives anything until it is confined. No Niagara is ever turned into light and power until it is tunneled. No life ever grows great until it is focused, dedicated, disciplined."

To accomplish IT and do IT well requires that every resource you have at your disposal be aligned with IT. Even if IT requires only five minutes to complete, being able to focus your physical, mental, emotional, and even financial energy effectively on IT for those few moments can have a major impact on getting IT done.

ORGANIZE AROUND **IT**

Just as a painter starts each painting with a blank canvas, start each of your days with a clean, organized mind, workspace, office, computer, computer files, e-mail box, and so on.

To accomplish IT and accomplish IT well requires that every resource you have at your disposal be aligned with IT.

Have you ever had to be out the door absolutely no later than a certain time early in the morning in order to be somewhere on time, and, as a result, you made sure everything was in place the night before? You laid out your clothes and double-checked the location of your car keys. You might have even loaded certain items into your vehicle so that all you had to do in the morning was dress yourself, eat, and launch yourself out the door. Every item was in place to ensure that you could leave (and therefore arrive) on time. It's necessary to use this same process while working to accomplish your highest priorities.

If much of your work on IT will take place in your workspace, determine whether it's organized toward helping you accomplish IT. It's easy to be distracted by memos, sticky notes with reminders on them, your in-box, your daily planner, or your computer. When you want to focus on IT, consider clearing away from your workspace everything that doesn't apply to IT. Put all distractions on the floor or behind you. Better yet, file everything in a way that enables you to put your hand on those items quickly if they might be needed for the present (or future) IT.

REMOVE DISTRACTIONS FROM IT

Funnels are naturally restrictive because of their shape. Our mental funnels sometimes are restrictive and resistant to allowing IT to flow through because something clogs them up. Removing such blocks from your mental funnel helps ensure the free flow of work on IT. Ask yourself, What's causing me to be distracted from working on IT? Most distractions fall into one of five categories:

- Physical. We mentioned items in your workspace that might need to be moved. Perhaps the area where you're working on IT is a little too hot or too cold, too noisy or too oppressively silent for comfort. Is it really that your energy level is too low for you to concentrate, or is the problem the stuffy air (lack of oxygen), the enormous sandwich you had for lunch (that relocates blood to your digestive system), or that ticking clock lulling you to sleep? Don't discount any physical element that could inhibit your work.
- Audible or Visible. Any external stimulus (e-mail notifications, your mobile phone, people passing by, unrelated papers or images in view) invites your brain to wonder, Should I be focusing on that instead of this? Remove all potential sources of distraction, or simply relocate yourself away from the distractions whenever possible.
- Financial. Hopefully, if your work on IT requires a temporary reduction in income (you're starting your own business or investing in new resources), you've taken steps to make up for the reduction. Perhaps you have secured a loan or found ways to cut back on

life expenses. If you haven't taken the steps to allow for an investment in IT, you'll find you're hemmed in by limited options. Instead, most every moment will be spent worrying about the cost of something you might genuinely need.

- Medical. Joe really wanted to start running with some of his friends on Saturday mornings. The social time with them was a big IT for him. Unfortunately, every time he ran more than a couple of miles his knees began to hurt and he would have to drop out of the group. Not wanting to abandon this IT, Joe talked with his doctor and found that a simple padded Velcro strap placed just below his kneecap prevented the pain from occurring. Joe is now running half marathons with his friends.

- Emotional. Is your distraction an unresolved issue with a coworker or family member? Maybe you have an incomplete task or unfulfilled obligation separate from your IT, and you keep punishing yourself for not working on that instead. Emotional distractions can take myriad deceptive forms and be especially hard to pinpoint and work out, but regardless of the nature of the emotional distraction, it might be preventing you from being fully focused on the IT that might bring you peace of mind.

Remember that IT is your first priority—that's the whole point. Instead of thinking of IT last, reflect on IT first and schedule the appropriate tasks and activities to achieve IT. That way, you're less likely to run out of time before you get around to IT.

Last, force yourself to complete one IT before taking on another one. With so much electronic and real-time communication vying for your attention, make yourself finish the task at hand before reading that e-mail, listening to your voice mail, or even having a conversation or meeting with someone. Deep, focused attention to IT is your best hope for completing IT effectively and efficiently instead of leaving IT unfinished and having to return to IT later—turning IT into yet another distraction preventing you from making progress on the next IT.

Beyond the Actual Plan

Now that we've addressed the dynamics of being organized and removing distractions, let's look at some key strategies to employ once you're in hot pursuit of IT.

MINIMIZE MULTITASKING

Multitasking is one of the most overused and misunderstood practices in the workplace nowadays. It originated as a computer-engineering term, and it's often touted as a way for people get more done in less time. People flaunt their ability to multitask—as if their job performance can be measured in floating-point operations per second—when, for human beings, dividing our attention can often be detrimental to our natural way of getting tasks done well, or at all.

Consider the following insights (and see if you can refrain from answering your phone, starting a conversation, or checking your e-mail while reading them):

Joseph T. Hallinan, the author of *Why We Make Mistakes*, writes: "There is no such thing as dividing attention between two conscious activities. Under certain conditions we can be consciously aware of two things at the same time, but we never make two conscious decisions at the same time. Try carrying on a conversation with your dinner guests while trying to figure the tip on the bill."

Even a computer slows its rate of work while multi-tasking (unless it has multiple processors). For humans, multiple processors would mean multiple brains. Interestingly enough, if you give a computer too many tasks, it starts "thrashing," which basically means it spends an overwhelming amount of time just trying to figure out how to organize the requests it's supposed to process and not actually completing any of them. Sound familiar?

A group of researchers from Stanford University made the following observation after a study on human multitasking: people who are regularly bombarded with several streams of electronic information do not pay attention, control their memory, or switch from one job to another as well as those who prefer to complete one task at a time. Eyal Ophir, a coauthor of the study, went on to say the subjects in the study "couldn't help thinking about the task they weren't doing. The high multitaskers are always drawing from all the information in front of them. They can't keep things separate in their minds."[1]

The air force attributes a significant number of its aircraft crashes to "task saturation." The term was coined to describe stress-based paralysis in aviators given too many tasks to complete at one time.

In a *Harvard Business Review* blog, Peter Bregman describes his research that exposes the serious downside of multitasking. He found that the IQs of people distracted by incoming calls and e-mails dropped by as much as ten points. That's a larger effect than losing a night's sleep and twice the effect of smoking marijuana. Productivity actually went down by as much as 40 percent due to time lost in "quick-switch tasking."[2]

Multitasking may sound like an effective way to work on IT, but don't be tempted. The end result is frequently time and energy wasted in jumping from one item to the next (and back), inhibiting your natural ability to focus intently on getting IT done.

MANAGE INTERRUPTIONS WHILE WORKING ON **IT**

One of the biggest laughs we experience in our training programs is when we ask people to raise their hands if they have too many interruptions. People will sometimes raise both hands.

Workflow interruptions are costly, especially when you're trying to accomplish it. In fact, an MIT study found that when employees are interrupted, they lose time and efficiency in two ways: First, the diversion itself takes them away from the task. Second, to get back into the task, they need to warm up their thinking again and refamiliarize themselves with where they left off.

We then ask a follow-up question: If we could find a way to take away all of your interruptions, how many of you would still have a job? Very few hands go up at that point. Most interruptions probably do have some connection to your work responsibility or personal values. To better manage your interruptions and minimize their impact, consider the following strategies:

- Review some reasons why other people interrupt you, and address their workflow habits before changing your own. Are the interruptions the result of people lacking information, knowledge, or skills that only you possess, a situation that could be easily corrected by documenting and distributing what you know? Are their requests similar, or are they the result of a variety of factors? If there's a pattern, what one change would eliminate a host of interruptions?

- Determine whether the interruption is important enough for you to change your current workflow. Does it qualify as an IT, or is it just something else? If the interruption is not dealt with now, will it create a larger problem in the future, leaving you less time for what you're trying to accomplish? Will handling this interruption help improve the productivity of other members of your team, allowing you to get more ITS done as well?
- Be less available when you want to focus on IT. Turn off e-mail notifications and send your phone calls directly to voice mail. Physically move out of an environment where you're frequently interrupted. Are you located near the break room or copier? Are you greeting countless people as they walk by? If so, and if you have a door, close it. If you're in a workspace with no door, post a red, yellow, or green sheet of paper where people stopping by will see it before they see your face. Explain to them that green indicates they're welcome to interrupt you for work-related matters, yellow means an interruption should be made only for an important reason, and red means not to bother you unless the building is on fire or you've won the lottery.

And When You Are Not the Boss . . .

A big "aha moment" comes in our training programs on time management when we direct participants to do the following: Think about the person who interrupts you most often. What percent of your daily workload do they understand? The answers range from 60 percent down to zero (yes, zero). Our next question is, If they have a limited understanding of at most 60 percent of your workload, why would they see a problem in interrupting you? The reality is they won't see an issue. How can they? They don't know all the tasks you are undertaking, and how full your schedule already is. And the person most commonly found doing the interrupting? The boss (or one of multiple bosses that exist in many of today's organizational structures).

A first step to help you focus on IT is to communicate your current workload to your supervisor or manager. Let them know how the work you are doing correlates to the highest priorities of your position and, hopefully, their expectations as well. Give them the consequences of your not being able to focus on IT.

Next, ask them how they would see you structuring your time to be better able to focus. Negotiate with them times of the day when you are most likely to be involved in high mental tasks that require focus and no interruption. Also discuss times that would be better for communication—like the end of the day. This exercise, when combined with the first step, will probably open their eyes to how their interruptions (and others) are affecting your work.

As you continue in the conversation, be ready to ask for resources to help you focus on IT. Do you always have to be at your desk, or can you work somewhere else from time to time where there are fewer distractions? Are there times of the day or week that you can block out to work on a specific task, and have the support of your boss in case someone wants to interrupt you?

Last, communicate the benefit to your boss and the goals of the work group or team if you are able to focus on IT more often. And thank them for their support. This discussion may not have been a planned IT for them and you want to ensure them that their time was well spent.

Measure Your Time on IT—or Not on IT

People who are successful at accomplishing what is most important don't have to guess where their time is spent. They know. They realize that spending time on the "right work" is key. A good way to measure where your time is spent (or not spent) is to use a time log for a week or two. It's a simple experiment. Just label the days of the week across the top of a spreadsheet and the time you want to track in fifteen- or thirty-minute increments (depending on how detailed you want to be) down the side. Set an alarm (your cell phone's alarm, watch alarm, or egg timer) for the top of each hour. When the alarm goes off (we realize this is an interruption, but the experiment is just for a week), stop what you're doing and record in detail what you've accomplished over the past hour—an entry for each fifteen- or thirty-minute segment. We realize this exercise is unnatural and a hassle, but the information you'll be gathering is likely to be very telling.

At the end of the week, review your activities. For fun, total the amount of time you spent in definable categories such as meetings, returning calls, writing e-mail, working on the XYZ report, talking with customers, eating meals, taking breaks, et cetera. You might be surprised at the totals. You might also be surprised at all the time you wasted. Be honest with yourself—look at the spreadsheet and total up the time you feel you've been less than productive. Have your team do the same.

Now what are you going to do about it? Ask yourself these questions:

- What activities are getting the bulk of my time? Are they IT for me by choice?
- How can I alter what I'm doing so that I'm spending more time on IT?
- What activities can be eliminated to allow more room for IT?

If you find this weeklong exercise helpful, try it for a month. It will give you a good indication of how effectively you're using your time and how much time you're actually devoting to your ITS. Remember what Ben Franklin wrote: "Dost thou love life? Then do not squander time, for that's the stuff life is made of."

Take Care of Yourself so You Can Take Care of It

In your drive to accomplish your IT, don't forget the one IT that should take precedence over many others: you! Take care of yourself so that you're in the best condition to accomplish IT. According to the Finnish Institute of Occupational Health (as reported by CNN), people who work ten to twelve hours per day are 56 percent more likely to develop heart disease or have a heart attack than those who work fewer than ten hours each day. They factored out stress, personality, and behaviors such as smoking. And take a look at these statistics, a bit closer to home, from the Families and Work Institute:

- 32 percent of Americans report that their work life has a primary negative impact on their lives off the job.
- Nearly two out of three individuals are overweight or obese.

- Nearly half (48 percent) of US employees have not engaged in regular physical exercise in the last thirty days.
- One third of the workforce shows signs of clinical depression.
- 39 percent of US employees took fewer vacation days than the number for which they were eligible (5 percent took none).[3]

To keep your body humming along and working at peak performance, keep these suggestions in mind:

- Set warning signals. It helps to have warning signals that tell you when you're working too hard or putting too much stress on your body. Some signals that change is needed might include:
  - skipping your personal time (reading, devotion, etc.) in the morning
  - telling yourself that you don't have time to exercise
  - failing to have at least two or three good laughs per day
  - feeling that you're "just going through the motions" at work
- Get enough sleep. When we're in the groove, we often tell ourselves, "If I could get one less hour of sleep, it would equate to an extra hour of productivity." Not so! Adults need an average

Take care of yourself so you can take care of IT.

of seven to eight hours of sleep each night. Don't shortchange yourself. You'll be less able to focus and you'll have less energy during the day if you don't get enough rest. Dr. Charles A. Czeisler, the Baldino Professor of Sleep Medicine at Harvard Medical School, reports, "The general effect of sleep deprivation on cognitive performance is well known: Stay awake longer than 18 consecutive hours, and your reaction speed, short-term and long-term memory, ability to focus, decision-making capacity, math processing, cognitive speed, and spatial orientation all start to suffer. Cut sleep back to five or six hours a night for several days in a row, and the accumulated sleep deficit magnifies these negative effects. (Sleep deprivation is implicated in all kinds of physical maladies, too, from high blood pressure to obesity.) People like this put themselves, their teams, their companies, and the general public in serious jeopardy."[4]

- Exercise. Walk, run, bike, do yoga, lift weights, swim, mountain climb . . . mix it up! Take care of yourself each day. Exercise is vital. Take care of the machine that's your body at least as regularly as you'd get oil changes and tune-ups for a vehicle you depend on.

- Take a break. Intense focus can be taxing and exhausting. You should have bursts or sprints of focus and productivity (no more than ninety minutes at a time) and then take a break. Step away, go for

a walk, stretch, take a five-minute power nap, get
a drink or eat a healthy snack, or stand outside and
look at clouds. Taking a break will help provide
you with the energy you need and can help you to
maintain your energy level later into the day.

- Watch what you eat. Yes, nutrition is important.
  It's part of watching your weight and making
  sure that you have the raw materials needed to
  generate energy for your day. If you're struggling
  to gag down that spinach or you're confused about
  what's nutritious and what isn't, read a book on the
  subject or, better yet, make an appointment with a
  nutritionist who can explain your choices. From a
  basic point of view:
  - Make sure you have a good breakfast to jump-
    start your day and your energy level.
  - Monitor the quality and quantity of your lunch.
    There is nothing worse than having a big lunch
    that brings you back to work lethargic and
    needing a nap. Keep lunch light and healthy.
    Save the burgers and fries for dinner or the
    weekend.
  - Consider energy foods throughout the day.
    Power bars, veggies, fruits, and nuts all can
    help boost your energy. Tie snacking with your
    break routine rather than waiting for big meals.
- Do more of the things you love. Line up your
  activities, and focus on the things you really enjoy.

Doing the things you enjoy builds positive-feedback routines and helps you maintain your energy level. If you're mostly doing things you don't look forward to, maybe it's time to look at what you're allowing to pass through your filter and how you set values on your goals. Spend more time on the things that rev you up and less time on the things that drag you down.

· Don't get discouraged! Overcoming self-destructive habits is hard work, but do you really prefer keeping them to making a little effort to form positive habits?

Yes, IT can force you to work hard. But that's what makes IT so valuable. Reflect on something tangible that you had to work really hard for or received because of a determined effort. Maybe it's a framed diploma, a letter of commendation from your boss, or a product prototype that you helped create. Perhaps it's a company policy or practice you drafted or helped develop as part of a team. Recall some pictures from a favorite vacation. Think about your children, your spouse, or your best friend (you might not recall all the hard work that went into building those relationships until you really go back into your memory).

Anything of lasting value in your life has no doubt required a considerable amount of effort. If it hadn't, it probably wouldn't have value to you. Consider what follow-up studies tell us about most people who win big in the lottery: before long, all their winnings are spent and it's hard for them to say where it went. "Easy come, easy go" happens to be true.

If it's hard for you to stay dedicated on your own, try building relationships with others who are also working hard on their ɪᴛs. They can readily relate to your struggle and often can share advice or tips. At the very least, others can help you realize that you're not the only person in the world with a hill to climb.

You Failed or Are Failing at Iᴛ

We could offer you the proverbial whack on the head at this point and list countless individuals who failed again and again, only to achieve their ɪᴛ eventually. Igor Stravinsky can speak for most of them: "I have learned throughout my life as a composer chiefly through my mistakes and pursuits of false assumptions, not by my exposure to founts of wisdom and knowledge." *The Rite of Spring* would eventually become Stravinsky's most famous work, but on May 29, 1913, when it debuted in Paris, the audience rioted! The unnatural choreography and unconventional music was just too much for many of those watching the performance. *The Rite of Spring* would later be credited with changing ballet forever.[5] Failure will happen—count on it. If it doesn't, you might not be attempting something of true worth to yourself or others.

Failing at something begins a process that forces you to clarify what you thought IT was and what you want IT to be. Use the process to give yourself data and direction on what you should do next to be successful with IT . . . or determine whether it needs to change.

And don't forget to be patient with yourself. Have the courage to look at yourself in the mirror and confront the faults that may have led to your failure with IT, and then do something about those faults. Find a possible solution, then patiently work toward improvement. It might be a daily battle for seemingly little progress, but the fight is worth it. In the end, you'll be a better you!

Fixed or Flexible Filters?

Do our filters ever change? Would a filter that is the most important one at one point ever become less important? The answer is yes!—especially over time and with age, wisdom, experience, finances, or a host of other factors. What happens when you're working hard to climb the ladder of success and find that your ladder is up against the wrong wall? What do you do? The biggest challenge may be determining if IT is truly the wrong IT or if you're just tired, bored, or unfocused.

Don't get discouraged!
Overcoming
self-destructive habits is
hard work.

If you have children, you've probably had experience with this concept. Especially if you "encourage" them to learn to play a sport or a musical instrument. Most all kids are excited at the idea of being on the football team or wearing the band uniform—or of scoring the winning goal or performing before screaming fans—but when it comes time to practice, the idea loses its appeal. You help out with gentle reminders and draw up practice charts. Then comes the nagging, the bribes, the threats. Eventually, there comes that moment of truth when, as a parent, you ask yourself, If I let her quit, am I teaching her how to be a quitter?

Todd knew a young man (we'll call him Patrick) who was an incredible high school athlete. He was a star basketball, football, and baseball player. He was a natural. His dad was his number one fan and also his very driven coach. Patrick's dad was passionate about sports and had Patrick practicing, attending clinics, and working aggressively on drills. The only problem was, Patrick wasn't passionate about sports. He had the natural talent and wanted to please his dad, but his real passion was music. He loved to play the guitar.

After a while, you could just tell from Patrick's attitude that he was unhappy playing sports because doing so kept him away from music. A big moment of truth came somewhere around Patrick's sophomore year. It seems Patrick reached a compromise with his father: Patrick could quit all the teams except one. He stayed with football until the end of high school, and he's still playing guitar and performing to this day.

The point is that you can have a talent for and be successful at a lot of things. It's not unusual for a person to be good enough at something that pays well to settle on it as a career—only to feel deeply unsatisfied later. Ideally, what makes us happy and what pays the bills coincide, but in the real world that's not always the case.

Sometimes we have to turn to a career where we can make a living even though our passion might be somewhere else. That's unfortunate and maybe even backward. The hope is that at least most of our ITS are tied to what we are passionate about.

The trick is getting past the hard work that leads us to the goal. Sometimes it's the passion that takes us there and gets us past the seemingly endless hours of practicing, training, studying, or working. That's why it's always good to pick something that we have passion for to help push us toward that goal. When times get tough and the work gets difficult, it's time to rekindle the passion.

Does the IT you're working on invoke passion or provide the resources to engage in your true passions? If the answer is no, then an intense search for a new IT may be in order.

As things change in your life, don't be afraid to have a flexible plan. Continually evaluate what you want to accomplish and what truly matters to you. New opportunities will come along. Follow your passion. Follow your gut. But the process remains true: Define IT, Focus on IT, and Accomplish IT.

Tired Yet?

If you ever meet Jones's friend Margaret, you'll be able to say you've met one of the most zany, energetic, charismatic, charming, and warm individuals in the world. She possesses tremendous organizational skills, plays the piano, directs choirs, and makes the world's most delicious homemade bread. She's a marriage and family therapist who has a beautiful way of helping people work through very difficult experiences. After a visit with Margaret, you can definitely say you've been in the presence of a "filler," an individual who always seems to know how to make us feel better about ourselves and to give us the encouragement to keep striving toward IT.

What you wouldn't know is that Margaret made the decision to go back to college and earn her degree in marriage and family counseling at age fifty-five . . . after she'd already been battling multiple sclerosis for several years. Her medication regimen is intense, and one can only imagine how hard it is for her some days just to get out of bed.

At her college graduation party, she shared with

us one of her secrets that kept her going toward her goal. She said, "Over the past four years I've had to put off a lot of what I wanted to do, or needed to do. My husband, Ed, and our kids pitched in to handle a lot of things that were my responsibility. Some things just plain never got done. It's hard for someone like me to admit I can't do everything. But I told myself, 'Fer cryin' out loud, Margaret, at least you can do this.'"

You probably know someone like Margaret: someone who doesn't get thrown off course by all the distractions life presents. Someone who has much bigger obstacles in her path than you have, and yet she does IT—one year (month, week, day, hour, minute) at a time. As you reflect on the Margarets you know, ask yourself, "Fer cryin' out loud, isn't there one IT I can start accomplishing right now?"

Chapter 7

After Accomplishing It

THE JOURNEY MAY BE MORE VALUABLE THAN
THE **IT** ITSELF.

Most ITS come with a deadline, a wrap-up, some type of completion. At some point, you've done IT, achieved IT, or become IT, and then you ask yourself, Now what? Rush on to something else? Return to what I was doing previously? Before you take on the next Important Thing, here are several things you might want to do to get the maximum benefit from the moment of accomplishing IT.

Celebrate and Reward Yourself

In chapter 5, Planning for It, we recommended creating an incentive or reward to draw yourself toward accomplishing IT—something you could focus on that would motivate you when the going gets tough. Once you accomplish IT, it's time to claim that reward. Don't shrug it off, don't shortchange yourself. Celebrate! If you deny yourself the reward you promised yourself, the next time you use this strategy to keep you going on your long "IT" adventure, it might not work.

In our Juggling Elephants training programs, we ask people who are struggling with too much to do about their "sense of accomplishment." The most common reply is, "There isn't any. I'm too busy moving on to the next thing." The despair in their voices is a good indicator of their lack of motivation to undertake the next IT with a fully charged sense of purpose.

As we discussed in chapter 5, pick a reward matched to what you have accomplished. If IT requires only a few minutes of mental or physical effort, consider rewarding yourself with a stretch break. If your IT is more challenging and requires a few hours of focus, consider taking care of some lesser tasks (taking out the trash, organizing a stack of paperwork) to remind yourself what a sense of accomplishment feels like.

Consider announcing your accomplishment to your coworkers or your family—or a complete stranger, for that matter! If you've communicated IT to others and drawn on them for support, they deserve to hear about ITS conclusion and celebrate with you. Those who encouraged you to believe in your own ability to accomplish IT might now feel encouraged to have their turn at saying "I did IT!" You're building positive reinforcement so that the next time you feel bewildered about how you're going to accomplish IT, or feel you're totally out of ideas, these memories of success—not failure—will rush in to fill the void.

Celebrate and Reward Others

When you accomplish IT alongside others, another critical step is to take a break and celebrate as a team. Otherwise, it's the sales manager mentality all over again: The last quarter's in the books. Now how are you going to meet next quarter's quota? The lack of even a moment of self-congratulation or an attitude of "Well, that's what you get paid for" can be demoralizing and sap everyone's will to go the extra mile next time. Most successful sales organizations truly get this strategy. They incentivize, they celebrate, they have rewards, they have trips, and they publicly recognize notable achievements.

Make a big deal about what has been accomplished. Few things are worse than arriving at the end of a project just to dive directly into the next one. We see too many individuals and organizations that simply won't take the time to celebrate—and their lack of enthusiasm to undertake a new IT anytime soon proves it. If you belong to a team or work for a boss who doesn't know how to celebrate, create your own personal

If you've communicated IT to others and drawn on them for support, they deserve to hear about ITS conclusion and celebrate with you.

celebration, even if it's after work. You earned the reward and you deserve to enjoy it.

A Caution About Rewards

In your excitement and planning, remember that there's more to a sense of accomplishment than just a tangible reward. We all have a built-in desire to do well. The engine for overcoming difficulty is part of our genetic makeup. A celebration can symbolize and thereby reinforce our natural need to start, dig at, and finish something. But if there's too much attention given to shiny medals, trophies, or bonus checks, our natural instinct for achievement might get pushed into the shadows; we risk conditioning ourselves and others to work for misguided reasons.

Rewards are important, but they don't need to get bigger every time something is accomplished. They function best when they are consistent, frequent, personal, and sincere. A study published in the *Journal of Personality and Social Psychology* found that people's satisfaction with their life-experience purchases, such as going to a movie or taking a vacation, tends to start out high and go up over time. On the other hand, although people might initially be delighted by that flashy new smartphone or the latest in fashion, their satisfaction with material purchases wanes with time. The study affirms what most of us already know: we like experiences that stay forever new in our memories better than material items that break or wear out.[1]

So recognizing the successful conclusion of IT with an event that celebrates our natural inner drive toward achievement, rather than focusing our desires on a shiny new sports car or corner office, is actually the best way to launch us toward the next IT.

Debrief—What Did You Learn?

The moment of bringing closure to IT is a good time to take stock of your achievement and what you've learned. If you feel let down or unmotivated, you may not have taken enough time for reflection in the past, perhaps because you were eager to get on with the next Important Thing. There is much to gain from reflection and consideration of what went well and what didn't, which steps were effectively planned and which were overlooked, on the path to accomplishing IT.

Reviewing a journal, pictures, logs, or the planning documents you've kept along the way is a good way to reflect on your journey. Reviewing your records after the fact can also reveal patterns you might not otherwise notice. While reflecting, consider questions such as these:

- What is the single biggest thing I learned during this process that I can apply to the future?

- What was the source of my greatest struggle?
- What can I do to better prepare myself, or my team, so that I don't face setbacks next time?
- What was an "aha moment" for me? What did I learn about myself?
- How could I have communicated better and gotten more people "on board"?

If others were involved in IT, get their observations and reflections as well. Enlightening questions could be:

- From your viewpoint, what could I have done better?
- What did you see me do that worked well or "seemed right"?

Wrap It Up

You have visualized, planned, created, shipped, and celebrated. Now it's time to close out your project. Don't leave unused building supplies and empty packaging just lying around on your formerly vacant lot, or fail to put that last brick in place.

Depending on the IT you just accomplished, this could mean archiving your files, cleaning up your workspace, donating clothes that are now too big, or throwing out unnecessary leftovers from your old IT so you can move to the next ITs on your list. Keep mementos,

The moment of bringing closure to IT is a good time to take stock of the achievement and what you've learned.

of course, but if you can't determine a useful purpose for some of the information or items created, at least put them where they won't distract you. Look ahead.

CREATE A PUNCH LIST

As you may know, construction contractors make punch lists—lists of all the little things that need to be wrapped up before closing out a project. The items on this list are usually the icing on the cake, the fine details that really put the finishing touches on the project. Items might include touching up paint on a bedroom wall, adjusting a cabinet door so it closes correctly, or straightening a light fixture in the bathroom. You should do the same with your IT. As part of your planning, make a punch list and finalize it so you don't keep adding trivial afterthoughts that drag out the conclusion of IT. When all items on the list are checked off, have a celebration—and move on.

DON'T RELAX TOO LONG

Once you've finished your punch list and are ready to move on, do just that . . . move! Don't rest on your laurels, spend your time reliving the glory days, and fall into stagnation. Clear your head to make room for your next IT. In fact, while that momentum and the discipline of focusing on IT are still in your routine, you should start operating your funnel and filters to determine what your next ITS are going to be.

Record the things you've learned in a log or journal so you can reference them the next time you take on a similar IT, or loan them to someone who's facing the same challenge.

Take an Intermission

It's important to clear your head and prepare for what's next. If your IT was to create a better filing system for your e-mail, you probably don't need to take the next week off to recover; however, if accomplishing your IT took a significant amount of time and energy (like completing an annual report for your department, remodeling a room, or losing twenty pounds), maybe it's time to step back so you can step forward. We call this "taking an intermission," and when you do take one, remember the Three R's:

- Rest. What type of rest is needed after accomplishing IT? Physical? Mental? Emotional? Financial? All four?
- Replenish. What elements of your life were depleted while you focused on your IT? Maybe you neglected your family, and now it's time for a weekend away. Perhaps you isolated yourself from some coworkers, and now they just need to know that you're still

among the living. Or it could be that you just need to catch up on your sleep! If long days and weekend work were necessary, take time to reconnect with those who have been patient with your focus. Include them in your celebration or in your intermission.

- Refocus. As you restore your energy and refresh your desire to tackle another IT, begin thinking about which IT should follow. We'll talk more about this in the next section.

One IT Leads to Another

As the glow from the successful IT begins to fade, it's time to review the possibilities in your funnel. Check your filters, make the necessary adjustments, prioritize your options, then proceed with your next IT. We'll discuss this step further in chapter 8, Doing It Again.

It's important to clear your head and prepare for what's next.

Chapter 8

Doing It Again

YOUR NEXT **IT** AWAITS.

If you've ever watched a movie with an epic battle scene, you know that as soon as the heroes conquer evil and begin to celebrate, some ember of the evil force rises from the ashes and regains its strength to come at them again. The time for celebration is then over, and it's back to the business of saving the world.

While you may not be engaged in a war against Orcs and Dark Wizards (although the Evil Urgent and the Devilish Unnecessary are battling to win out against your Heroic It), you know the next Important Thing awaits. Your workday, your relationships, and even your waistline demand an ongoing series of ITS. Get IT right most of the time, and the likelihood of success is greatly magnified. Allow everything else constantly to take precedence over your most promising options, and you risk losing IT.

Another variation of this theme is to consider the story of Sisyphus in Greek mythology. You may remember from English class that King Sisyphus ruled his kingdom with an iron fist and was very clever in dealing with the gods. He angered Zeus because he told the river god Asopus the whereabouts of his daughter, Aegina, and killed many of those traveling through his kingdom. As punishment for his behavior, King Sisyphus was forced to carry or roll a giant boulder up a steep hill. When he was about to reach the top of the hill the massive stone would roll back down and he would be forced to start all over again. He was resigned to an eternity of hopeless hard work and unrelenting disappointment.

Could that be a description of your modern-day life? As a caregiver of children, do you labor all day to clean, organize, and pick up after others, just to wake up in the morning having to start all over again? As a worker, do you spend the majority of the day reading, organizing, and responding to e-mail, just to show up the next day and find another fifty e-mails in your inbox to be dealt with?

If you have a routine, is the routine going to help you meet your goals over time? Are you swimming toward a destination, or are you just treading water? How do you make sure you are pointed in the right direction and that you are focused on the right things?

Whether IT is a task tied to your life's purpose (such

as a career choice or change) or simply the choice of how to spend the next three minutes, there are times when you might have to reevaluate your thinking, realign your plans, or possibly even redefine your IT. In nautical terms, it's a course correction—sometimes toward a completely new destination.

It would be nice if we were born with a map that lays out, year to year (or maybe even month to month), precisely what we should focus on at each stage of our lives to take a straight-line path to success, happiness, and great achievements. As convenient as that might sound, we all know that that would take all the fun out of life. Looking back at our footsteps, we'd see an awful lot of meandering, though there's nothing necessarily regrettable about that; life's not about finding the most direct path between cradle and grave. Even so, a compass would sure come in handy now and then.

Once you've successfully accomplished an IT, you probably have a clearer idea of where you want to go next, and you've equipped yourself with valuable tools to guide you efficiently. You just have to answer, What's my next IT?

What Have I Neglected While I've Been Focusing on It?

When you move an IT out of your funnel, process it, and check it off your list, you're ready to sort through new possibilities and select your next Important Thing. Before you move too quickly, however, reflect on the possibilities that have been in your funnel for some time, waiting for their chance. Which opportunities can you now move along into your action plan, and which no longer belong?

One of the most frequent reflections we hear from individual clients is the need to focus on relationships. In our quest to conquer professional goals and climb the ladder of success, our families and friendships often bear the sacrifice. It is time to increase your level of involvement with those who are most important to you—a growing child, an aging parent, a spouse who has patiently guarded the castle while you were off slaying dragons.

*Review Your Funnel and Filters That Help You Determine I*ᴛ

You might not want to assume that you know what your next Important Thing should be. If you've established an effective method for reviewing your funnel and filters for your day or week, you probably know what item should become ɪᴛ. But you might not want to engage in the next action until you've given yourself a chance to review your situation.

Assumptions can get you into a lot of trouble. A few years ago, Jones secretly planned a surprise day out

What have I neglected while I've been focusing on IT?

for his wife, Lisa, and her best friend, Abby. He had Lisa believing that Abby was going to stay with the children while he and Lisa went out. When Abby arrived, Jones led them both out the door and told Lisa, "Surprise! You're spending the day with Abby!" Jones said the look he got from his wife would have shattered glass. He later learned she was upset because they hadn't been out on a "date" together for quite a while, and she'd been really looking forward to spending time alone with him. Jones is usually sensitive to such things, but this time he just missed it. If he had taken a few minutes to review his funnel, he would have realized how much time he'd been spending apart from Lisa. Instead, he misdirected his effort to arranging her surprise day out with her friend.

If you're looking at your next big IT, consider giving your attention first to your values, beliefs, and priorities filters. Nowadays, parents often devote a lot of time and effort during their children's secondary-school experience and even into their college days to helping the children sort through their priorities and define what they want to be when they grow up. Unfortunately, much less time and attention is devoted to defining what they want to be *as* they grow up.

In *The Art of Virtue*, Benjamin Franklin wrote that he chose twelve virtues that he wanted to embody in his life: temperance, silence, order, resolution, frugality, industry, sincerity, justice, moderation, cleanliness,

You might not want to assume that you know what your next IT should be.

tranquility, and chastity. Each one was an IT for him, and he worked on one each week.

While reviewing your filters, ask yourself, like Franklin did, which of your virtues are weak or need extra attention? Don't put off the opportunity to concentrate on the deeper and richer things in life. You can be constantly busy checking items off your to-do list, or you can spend a little of your time on something that really adds value and meaning to your existence.

Consider the midlife crisis. We've all heard of it, and some of us have experienced it. A midlife crisis can occur when an individual comes to grips with his mortality and/or determines that he feels as if his life is half over and he's not sure what he has accomplished. This can sometimes result in making poor choices or focusing on activities that are not in line with one's values and goals (e.g., new sports cars, extreme adventures, "trophies" of the wrong kind). On the other hand, it can become a time of reflection when an individual realizes that his filters have become clogged, foggy, loosely defined, or mentally outdated compared to the present situation he finds himself in.

It's easy to become so busy in the first half of your life getting "stuff" done that you neglect to stop and intentionally evaluate where you are and what you want to achieve of value going forward.

Empty nesters often struggle with the next IT. These are parents who have devoted much of their lives to the

monumental IT of raising children. They've focused all
their effort—every waking moment of every day—on
the myriad responsibilities of family life and have ignored or postponed other ITS that could be important
to them: nonfamily relationships, hobbies, undeveloped
talents, or dreams. Suddenly, the children are grown up
and on their own, and the parents don't know what to
do next; it's like falling off a cliff. It's not uncommon for
marital friction, sometimes even resulting in divorce, to
arise at this stage of life, simply because the couple isn't
prepared for what happens after such an all-consuming
IT reaches its conclusion. Other life junctions—
retirement, the death of someone close, the loss of a job,
the sale of a business—often present similar challenges.

To ensure that you are continually aligned with
your values and goals, ask yourself some of the following questions:

- What circumstances or conditions are different
  than they were one year ago? Six months ago? Two
  weeks ago? If you're working on a short-term IT,
  you may actually need to look at what has changed
  in the past thirty minutes. It could be a stockbroker
  watching the market, a motivational speaker taking
  stock of the energy level of her audience, a teacher
  adjusting a lesson plan after a fight at recess. The
  key is to be aware of how possibilities in your funnel
  may have changed based on these conditions.

- Based on these changing circumstances or conditions, what new goals, opportunities, or passions do I need to consider now to determine what IT will be for me?
- Are my daily activities fulfilling my needs?
- Is my focus on a major IT (such as raising children) causing me to neglect other areas (such as my relationship with my spouse or taking care of myself)?
- Am I moving forward, staying the same (getting stale), or moving backward (regressing)? Ask this question as it relates to work, relationships, and your personal well-being.

The value of a course correction or adjustment cannot be overstated. In fact, the busier you are, the more important it is to take stock of the conditions around you and see how they affect your choice of IT. Remember: the *Titanic* sank in large part because it was moving so quickly that it could not make changes in time to avoid the iceberg.

Being off course by just a small degree can make a big difference. In 1979, a passenger jet with 257 people on board left New Zealand for a round-trip sightseeing flight to Antarctica. Unbeknown to the pilots, someone had accidentally modified the stated flight coordinates by a mere 2 degrees. This error placed the aircraft 28 miles (45 km) to the east of where the pilots assumed

The value of a course correction or adjustment cannot be overstated.

they were as they approached Antarctica. The pilots descended to give the passengers a better look at the landscape. Although both pilots were experienced, neither had made this particular flight before, and they had no way of knowing that the incorrect coordinates had placed them directly in the path of Mount Erebus, an active volcano that rises from the frozen landscape to a height of more than 12,000 feet (3,700 m). The snow that covered the volcano blended in with the white clouds through which they were flying. By the time the plane's instruments sounded the warning that the terrain was rising up in front of them, it was too late for the pilots to make an adjustment. The aircraft crashed, and all 257 people onboard were killed. All because they were off course by just 2 degrees.[1]

Though that's an extreme example, it goes to show that it doesn't take much for you to get off course. Even a few degrees (or distractions) can make a big difference in where you are on the path toward your goal.

Improving on the Possibilities That Become It: Continuous Progress

Another step in the process of preparing to do IT again is to look at the big picture. In vacant-lot terms, you're no longer looking just at your lot, you're looking at the changing conditions of your block, and even your community, that could signal a need to rethink your landscape design. To better address what might need to be improved upon, consider the following six-step process:

1. Identify areas for improvement. Based on facts, feelings, or insight you have at hand, what new possibilities may need to be included in your funnel? What possibilities are missing? List them. Be specific regarding your work, your relationships, and your personal well-being.
2. Gather feedback. Determine sources of feedback on how you're currently doing in these areas. You might be surprised to discover what others see as your strengths compared to areas in need of possible improvement. Don't rule out formal assessments, checklists, and other practical tools that can help you assess your situation.
3. Determine critical areas of improvement based on valid feedback. "Critical areas" are the possibilities that are most in line with your more important filters, such as your values and goals. "Valid feedback" is that which you've corroborated with more than one source.
4. Plan for improvement in your daily routine. What possibilities need to become IT for you in the next day or week? Maybe some new IT needs to become part of your routine. You might refer to this type of IT as "perpetual," because it needs to be undertaken

and completed every day. Examples include daily exercise, recordkeeping, or spending time with a loved one.

5. Measure results, and return to Step 1. How will you measure the benefit of having this new IT as part of your blueprint?

6. Ask for ideas on the next IT. If you've established a strong connection with people who are clearly focused on accomplishing their IT, you should have no trouble obtaining new possibilities from their example. Sometimes a fresh point of view, a differing opinion, or a recommendation can be just what you need to jump-start your next IT.

TED (originally an acronym for technology, education, and design) is a good example of a forum for sharing new ideas. Started in 1984 as a conference of "ideas worth spreading," the nonprofit organization has grown to include events around the world and in cyberspace with one goal: to improve the lives of others and, ultimately, the world, by spreading innovative ideas. Numerous big ideas have come out of the events over the years; their Web site (www.ted.com) is a rich resource if you're looking for new possibilities to consider.

You also might want to plan and work on an IT with someone else; you'll not only expand your horizons, you might develop a valuable new relationship. You might

Sometimes a fresh point of view, a differing opinion, or a recommendation can be just what you need to jump-start your next IT.

choose to take a class together, work on a book together, volunteer together, or work on a healthier lifestyle together.

Consider What Is Lacking in Your Life Right Now

Rarely is a decision made that doesn't affect other decisions yet to be made.

Consider Katie, a manager whose IT over the course of a few weeks is to train a newly hired coworker. Once Katie finishes working closely with the new hire (presumably, when the new employee is able to work independently), Katie's next IT might be to reconnect with her other coworkers and spend a little more time with them to catch up on what she's missed.

If you've been working hard, running children here and there, attending to the needs of everyone else and not taking time for yourself, your next IT might be to plan a day of "me" time, during which you do something you enjoy—enjoy a day at the spa, watch a favorite movie, or loosen up your golf swing. Here are some questions to help you determine whether matters you'd normally consider trivial have grown enough in importance to qualify as your next IT:

• Where have my time and energy been focused lately?

- If I had to choose three things that I have neglected recently, what would they be? Which people or processes have slipped out of my normal routine?
- How soon do I need to give more of my attention to these neglected items?

A Mental Crossroads

Kaizen, meaning "improvement," is a Japanese word that has become part of the vocabulary of business-people globally. It refers to a method for achieving quality and efficiency improvements in manufacturing, engineering, administration, and management processes. Typically, *kaizen* improvements occur gradually, in small increments, as opposed to the kind of top-to-bottom, radical-change campaigns that corporate executives are fond of launching but that often invite resistance from rank-and-file workers. Many studies have proven that the *kaizen* method—involving a feedback loop of constant adjustments and attention to even minute problems—results in much more significant and lasting improvements over time than conventional command-and-control programs.

Robert Maurer brings the *kaizen* strategy out of the corporate environment and into our personal lives in his book *One Small Step Can Change Your Life*, in which he makes the case that each of us can use "baby

What small things, done over time, can make a big difference in your life or the life of someone else?

steps" to accomplish far-reaching improvements in our own lives.

People often jump to the conclusion that an Important Thing has to be a major change or giant project. *Kaizen* illustrates that this doesn't need to be the case. Ask yourself what small adjustments, repeated and amplified over time, might make a big difference in your life or the life of someone near you.

A colleague recently described a small act of kindness his mother did for him every day before he went to school. As if her preparing a homemade lunch for him every day for thirteen years wasn't enough personal attention, she also always wrote a note to him on the napkin she included in his lunch bag—just a brief message reminding him how much she loved him and telling him to have a great day. Thirty years later, with a tear in his eye and a lump in his throat, this grown man swears those lunches and notes account for what he is today—a confident and successful businessman. No matter what terrors, disappointments, and temptations confronted him in the course of a school day, he always knew that he was loved and that everything would turn out okay.

The title of this chapter is Doing It Again. The exciting—and, yes, even scary—concept is that you are ultimately the one who decides what you will accomplish and focus on. It really is up to you (no pressure). This is not easy stuff! We find that, on average, only 10 to 20 percent of individuals actively write down their goals and formally focus on how to improve their situation. Whether your next IT is a baby step or an astronomical leap, don't sit back and watch your life go by. Seize the moment, hour, week, and year to accomplish what is important to you and those around you.

Chapter 9

Working with Others on It

IS SOME PART OF YOUR **IT** ALSO AN **IT** FOR THEM?

In chapter 7, After Accomplishing IT, we focused on getting support for your work on IT. You may look at the title of this chapter and ask, Isn't this the same thing? The answer is no. Getting others to support you is one thing. Getting them to change their attitudes or behaviors and actively participate in accomplishing a shared IT is quite another matter.

To better establish the need to get others to work with you on IT, reflect on the activities you have planned for the next twenty-four hours. Consider writing them in the margin of this page. If you already have them written down, review them.

Now ask yourself: How many of my ITS will require one or more of the following?

- working with others to change a policy, procedure, or method of doing business
- uniting and/or combining the talents of a team, department, company, or family
- developing a new skill by you and your coworkers
- planning an overnight camping trip for a group of Boy or Girl Scouts
- creating a plan as a family to tackle spring cleaning after a long winter
- leading others into "uncharted waters" or uncertain change
- modifying a process or product in which others have invested a great deal of their time and/or energy

Unless you're living on a desert island with no one to answer to but yourself, most ITS will require some level of "buy in" or participation from others. Fail to get other people to change, and the IT you're working on may remain unnecessary, misguided, or even threatening in their hearts and minds. And without the participation of others, it might mean that you end up doing all of the work yourself (remember your funnel is already really full). So how do you lead others to and through IT?

Consider an analogy: Suppose the quarterback of a football team has a fantastic idea of how to beat the defense and score a touchdown. The only problem is that he didn't think of IT until after the huddle. He could call

*Most ITS will require
some level of "buy in" or
participation from others.*

a time-out or an audible (that is, call out the new play to teammates just before the snap of the ball), but he decides to run the play on his own. The ball is snapped, and he executes his part brilliantly—but the play fails because no one else knew where he was headed or which of the opposition to block. Was his idea a bad one? No, it could have worked beautifully. The bad part was not sharing the plan with those around him in a timely manner so they could all coordinate their actions.

Now let's change the scenario: The quarterback reads the defense, calls a time-out, and explains the new play to the team. The linemen are clear on their roles, the receivers know exactly what to do, and the fullback understands the quarterback's expectations perfectly. The ball is snapped, all players execute just as expected, and a touchdown is scored on the play. The quarterback becomes a hero in less than a minute—all because he communicated IT.

Who needs to know about and contribute to your work on IT?

Remember, We're All Multiple Property Owners

We have referred to your vacant lot throughout this book. If you think about it, though, you actually own more than one lot. You have your very own lot, and much of what you do with it is up to you. Others may help create something on it, but the lot is yours. You also have a partial deed to a number of other lots. Along with your coworkers, you own a piece of property on which you can build something fantastic on . . . or on which you can simply allow weeds to grow. You and your family members also own a piece of real estate where you can build something of great value.

As you reflect on what these lots should become, try not to assume that others will immediately grab their hard hats, gloves, and tools to help you make IT successful. You may have thought a lot more about the possibilities and what IT should be than they have. Communication, again, is key.

Encourage Feedback and Ideas on How to Accomplish IT

When individuals are asked for input on how a community lot—a neighborhood vegetable garden, a local park—should be changed, they develop a sense of ownership and engage more fully in making IT successful. A bit of strategy might be needed at this point. Although you may already have the end result in mind, asking questions and synthesizing responses allows others to come to the same conclusion. The process of collectively reaching the same conclusion can be so much more effective than simply telling the team, "Here's the objective and here's how we're going to do it." Working together on the strategies, tactics, and outcomes creates buy-in that's crucial to success. You also might be pleasantly surprised as new and even better ideas are brought to the table.

Agree on Funnels, Filters, and the Sensible Vision

As you continue moving forward to build an IT on these "community" lots, review with your team members the process that brought this IT to the forefront for you, and get their input to determine the best course of action. Some guiding principles might be:

- When individuals are asked for input on how a community lot should be changed, they develop a sense of ownership and engage more fully in making IT successful.
- What outcome are we looking for from our actions as a team/department/family? Find agreement before moving forward.
- Based on that outcome, what are our options? If people are slow to share ideas, offer those you've identified as a starting point, but don't offer them as the only possibilities. When you've narrowed the options to three or four, move to the next step.
- Decide which criteria should be used to determine what the next step or steps should be.

- Get consensus on IT based on the agreed-upon criteria.
- Build a sensible vision around IT. What will be the milestones? What will be the end result? What are the resulting benefits? Success should have a tangible benefit for every person who works on IT.
- Visualize the advantages of accomplishment. Ask how the workday will be different or how the family environment will be better or how the organization will benefit, and determine tangible ways that the participants will be able to recognize the value of this new direction. Use pictures, charts, or banners to help people visualize what success will look like.
- Create a plan to accomplish IT as a team.

We recommend using the Six S strategy to create an action plan that best accomplishes IT:

- *Seek* out the strengths of those on your team.
- *Set* clear expectations. Don't be ambiguous. Clearly describe each individual's responsibility, actions that need to be taken, and the desired outcome from those actions.
- *Search* for opportunities to stretch others.
- *Schedule* clear deadlines: What is to be completed in what form, by whom, by when?
- *Synchronize* goals, outcomes, and values that will

eliminate or at least minimize activities that don't fully contribute to achieving the desired end.

- *Sustain* a focus on IT—keep the "heat," the sense of urgency, simmering through strong communication and firm accountability.

Let's return to the vacant-lot analogy. Consider that progress on your lot is humming along nicely—until your finance person says you're overbudget. One contractor hasn't shown up in two weeks, and you're at risk of not meeting one of your deadlines. The plumber and the electrician are arguing incessantly. You could just quit. Stop the project. Send all the workers home and tell the bank you've changed your mind. See if the local building-supply company will give you a refund on those "slightly used" nails. Think they would understand?

Roadblocks and obstacles are inevitable when working with others. You can quit, or you can find a way to succeed. You and your team are likely to realize you've all put too much time and energy into this IT simply to walk away.

Even with advanced preparation and planning, people may still have trouble staying focused and being effective as a team. Remember that you're reading this book because something always seems to get in the way of your ITS. Even though you've worked together with others to reach consensus on IT and you've secured their buy-in, something undoubtedly will try to sneak into their schedules and supplant work on IT. To minimize this danger, some additional upfront guidelines might be helpful:

- Put a system in place for people to regularly report progress along the way.
- Build accountability for everyone. Spell it out, and reinforce how someone's failure to work on IT affects others. Better yet, have them spell it out for one another and for themselves. This will ensure that recognition of the need for accountability is shared.
- Define well in advance what constitutes genuine grounds for adjustment of IT.
- Encourage and build formal collaboration between individuals and teams to ensure that they are and remain in sync about IT.
- Agree on what appropriate feedback looks like. Doubts, alternative ideas, and second thoughts ought to be offered and worked through early in the process; nitpicking or grumbling by those who show up late to the party and don't really understand IT should be defused immediately.

*Other Challenges That Come When Working with Others on I*T

Here are some examples of further challenges that may emerge when working with others on IT.

GETTING EVERYONE ON BOARD

When discussing change within an organization, we invariably get the question, How much time should I spend trying to get someone on board with a new idea? It's a good question. Contemplate your answers to the following questions to see if you have done your due diligence in getting others to buy in to IT:

- Have I clearly communicated a realistic vision of IT, demonstrating ITS benefit to the person, to his/her position in the organization, and to the continued health and growth of the organization?
- Have I made available to the person resources to upgrade his or her skills, and channels through which to share concerns and/or provide feedback? Have I given him or her tools and resources necessary to be successful?
- Have I established the real and concrete dangers of not attempting to accomplish this IT?
- Have I shown this person examples of how similar ITS have been successful in this or other organizations?

If the answer to most of these questions is yes and you still face resistance from people to your IT, then you might have to continue without their full support, whether they like it or not. But think of this as a last, highly undesirable resort, and keep in mind that the real world seldom presents all-or-nothing situations. If full support is out of the question, how about partial support? Or at least the person's word that he or she won't stand in the way of the project?

COMMUNICATION, COMMUNICATION, COMMUNICATION

Is there such a thing as too much communication? In most cases, especially where collaboration is concerned, the answer is no. In fact, lack of communication is the major reason that working on IT as a team fails. Most people would rather get too much information about the progress being made on an IT than feel left in the dark or left out of the loop.

We've already emphasized the importance of getting others to agree to contribute to the completion of IT at the outset: it's important for team members to understand why they should be focusing on IT and what's in IT for them. Once you've reached consensus on the vision and everyone is aligned, good communication throughout the process is essential. Continual discussion, regular progress reports, and deadline reviews are important to maintaining excitement and focus— and ensuring IT gets done!

COLLABORATION AND THE LACK THEREOF

We've already discussed the importance of assigning responsibilities and defining each team member's role in accomplishing IT so members as individuals are ready to shoulder their separate responsibilities. That said, it's still important to encourage collaboration and sharing. The worst thing that can happen is for everyone to go back to their silos and work on IT as if no one else were involved—without cohesion. This is why coming together for regular project updates and reviews throughout the process is vital.

MANAGEMENT BY COMMITTEE

Generally speaking, no brilliant decisions are made when everyone has an equal say. When there are strongly held, disparate opinions, a final decision can be reached only by watering down the results to a least-common-denominator level of agreement or by wearing down resistance until an "I don't care—just tell me what to do and I'll do it" attitude yields weak (and usually temporary) authority to the dominant personality. Unless there is authentic, carefully cultivated consensus—grounded in everyone's awareness of the risks of not setting aside disagreements in the end—management by committee is a very shaky form of management.

There are, no doubt, cases where true leadership must be exerted when consensus is stymied. Abraham Lincoln is said to have polled his cabinet (and included his own vote) on an issue where he sensed strong opposition. "Seven nays, one yea," Lincoln announced. "The yeas have it."

SCOPE CREEP

If you've done a good job of setting expectations, scope creep—the endless moving back of the goalpost—should not be a major issue. If it does become an issue, see if you can define where one IT stops and another IT begins. Reach agreement early on how best to establish the point of closure with one IT (so you can celebrate, review, etc.) before moving on to the next IT. Don't be afraid to say, "We will include that in version 2.0. But for now, let's keep to the plan."

EXECUTION

Difficulty with the execution of IT is often a given rather than an exception. Connect as often as possible with those working on IT, and ask specific questions about progress. If responses are vague and there's a sense that key tasks are getting stuck, turn your attention to the "something elses" that might be getting in the way of IT. If you can help teammates better manage those detours and distractions, offer assistance. If you're in a position with enough authority to banish side issues, don't hesitate. If the culprit is a team's or team member's poor work habits, you might offer solutions from chapter 6, Doing It, and from your own experiences. Watch for those who are falling behind or hindering the progress of others, hold them accountable, and give added support and resources where necessary. Milestones and deadlines are always helpful in encouraging execution; things with an inviolable due date attached tend to get done.

OTHER PEOPLE MAY NOT WANT TO GET **IT**

Even if you're consistent with your words and actions, there's a chance not everyone will want to follow your lead. Some people might be jealous of your success because you consistently get your Important Things done. Your success with IT could remind them of their own past failures to complete their own ITS or instead simply to act with purpose.

Jones was working with an HR director who was trying to identify ways to get employees on board with a specific change in the manufacturing workflow (the IT of the moment at her corporation). Jones's one question was, "What are they seeing or hearing that gives them faith the change will happen?" When she answered, "Nothing," Jones replied, "Well, then you don't really know for certain if they're for or against the change. They're waiting to see if you are serious about making the change."

While working with the Who Moved My Cheese? organization, we were continually amazed at how people could quickly see their own reasons why change was needed but were often blind to why others had a different perspective. Know that, regardless of how well you feel you've communicated IT, others may be less impressed with your reasoning. Your IT just might not be their IT, no matter how well you've communicated your point of view.

You also can view the situation surrounding IT as if it were a ball rolling downhill. When people see you charging in (riding on IT), they have three choices: they can get out of your way as you fly by; they can stand resolutely in your way and get run over; or they can start running, catch up to you, and take the journey with you. We should always work toward the last of those three while understanding that either or both of the first two may occur, unfortunately. Even though you bring clarity to others' willingness to buy in to IT, they won't always be happy about every aspect of the process. And there are some people who invariably, unshakably, irrationally resist change; they prefer the status quo or fear instability and don't like to leave their comfort zone.

What do you do when you get pushback from others because of conflicting ITS or because they just don't connect with your IT? Consider employing the Seven Steps for Reconnecting Them to Your It to keep things moving along:

1. Ask for their help directly.
2. Give a nonthreatening description of the situation from your perspective that invites their advice.
3. Explain how the situation makes you feel.
4. Ask about the effect if the current course of action continues.
5. Ask for their "outsider" perspective.
6. Determine points of agreement rather than disagreement.
7. Indicate your willingness to choose a new course of action based on discussion.

Wrapping It Up with Others

In chapter 7, After Accomplishing It, we discussed the importance of properly wrapping IT up once you've finished IT. This is especially true when working on IT with others. Attending meetings during the execution of IT can be so tedious and annoying that it's easy to skip yet another meeting once IT has been completed and simply move on to the next project without regard for what you all have just accomplished and learned.

Remember these steps for wrapping up IT when you've been working with others:

Your IT just might not be their IT, no matter how well you've communicated your point of view.

CELEBRATE AND REWARD THE TEAM

In the planning process, you will have decided on a meaningful celebration and reward at the end to help keep the group driving toward completion. Now that you've accomplished IT, keep that promise you all made to one another. Memories of that celebration of closure will help your team members the next time they're heavily engaged in an IT and need some "carrot" to keep them plodding forward.

REVIEW AND LEARN FROM **IT**

It's important to sit down and formally review the IT you've all just completed. What went right? What went wrong? Don't be so eager to "strike the set" and pack everything away (as cast members do on the closing night of a play) that you don't take time for learning. Preserve and review any project plans or records the team kept during the process. Ask one another: Based on this experience, what would you do differently in the future?

CLOSURE

When IT is completed, close out the project in no un-certain terms. In chapter 7, After Accomplishing It, we recommended making a final punch list in advance for IT. Do the same with your team. Assign final tasks, and formally declare the project complete once they're accomplished. Encourage archiving files and sorting through leftover materials, storing this for future use, discarding that . . . but don't linger too long on this process—set a postdeadline deadline. Once you've finally declared it done, don't savor your achievements so long that everyone forgets the feeling of being in the throes of a battle with an uncertain outcome; rather, put IT behind and align everyone to move forward to the next Important Thing.

DOING **IT** AGAIN

You most likely have a long list of ITs waiting their turn. The completion of an IT, especially a major IT, is a good time to review your organization's, department's, and/ or your own professional funnel and filters. What has changed as a result of accomplishing IT? Is there a need to reprioritize or rethink your long-term strategy? What did you learn about your team members as they focused on the last IT? Maybe it's time to do some promoting or coaching so the next IT goes even smoother?

It is also important to remember that failing at IT as a team, family, or group of friends can have more impact than just the typical hard costs of the failure or loss of time spent. There is a psychological cost as well. If a project fails, those who have been working on IT with you are going to be less likely to work on IT with you again. Following the strategies outlined above can not only influence the success of accomplishing the current most Important Thing but also future Important Things.

"I'd Be Dead in the Water Without Them"

In 2007 there was a strike by Hollywood's writers that went on for many weeks. Among those affected were late-night-TV talk-show hosts. As the strike wore on, people questioned why improvisational masters like David Letterman and Jay Leno couldn't continue their shows without writers. Jon Stewart renamed his show *A Daily Show* rather than *The Daily Show* as a tribute to the writers who made the show successful. Leno gave the answer—obvious to everyone who works on such a production, if not to the audience—when he said, "I'd be dead in the water without them. They make me who I am."

You could make a similar comment about your work on IT. Although there might be a few cases where you could pull IT off without the support and assistance of others, most of the time you severely limit your chances of being successful with IT without the full support of a team, whether they're your coworkers, your family, or a close circle of friends.

You severely limit your chances of being successful with IT without the full support of a team.

Chapter 10

Wrapping It Up

A SUCCESSFUL LIFE IS A SUCCESSION OF
SUCCESSFUL **ITS**.

Envision what your work and life would be like if you could fully focus on IT, the most Important Things, all the time. At work, you'd find that you accomplish what is most important rather than being constantly distracted by nonessentials. You're not working in a thrashing, "everything's a crisis" mode, but when a true crisis does arise, you deal with it efficiently and get right back to IT.

You are regularly cognizant of what is in your funnel and utilize your filters to find the best selection of and timing for your tasks. Interruptions still attempt to derail your day, but you manage them more effectively. You find that you rarely feel like you're working all alone. Your ability to clearly communicate goals and priorities to those around you has teams assisting, focusing, and executing IT.

In chapter 5, Planning for It, we discussed the law of inertia and the large amount of energy required to get the ball rolling. With the clarity and energy IT offers, you're probably moving more quickly than ever toward the right destinations. Simply put, when you're focused on IT, you're working on the right things, at the right moment, in the right place.

The benefits may not stop there. Your relationships become stronger. Before you began this journey of ITS, you often felt as if those you care about most got only your leftovers. Now they benefit from more time, and higher-quality time, with you. Having recognized the need to shed some negative relationships, you've also improved your ability to build strong bonds with the people who sincerely want to see you accomplish IT.

And look at you! While defining IT, you realized that part of your frustration was that you were allowing irrelevant urgencies and misdirected worries to stand in the way of your own personal growth and well-being.

Things are different now. Your physical, mental, emotional, spiritual, and even financial conditions are much better than they were just a few short months ago.

It's important to remember that you might not have achieved a specific IT yet—that could still be years in the future—but there are obvious benefits and rewards that come with checking off milestones along

Focusing on and achieving your Important Thing is a process . . . one that never ends.

the way. Focusing on and achieving your Important Thing is a process . . . one that never ends.

Some Final Thoughts About It

Our driving passion for writing this book grew out of a need both of us recognized to develop a way to stay focused in an unfocused world. It was a commitment to make sure we didn't miss work-related opportunities, naturally. But our families and personal relationships are big filters in our lives as well, and we didn't want to be squandering opportunities to enjoy every possible moment with them. We're not getting any younger, and we both had come to realize that failure to give attention to what's important tomorrow and the next day can add up to a lifetime of regret.

A second, and perhaps more compelling, reason for putting down in writing what we were discovering was to help others answer their own question, How am I going to live? They simply might not know how to cut through the "thick of thin things" and get to what matters most to them. There may be people who are satisfied with a life of trivialities; they'll continue to punch the clock, aimlessly surf the Web, play solitaire, mow the lawn, and be content settling into what Theodore Roosevelt called "the gray twilight that knows neither victory nor defeat." This book is not for them.

Another of our reasons for setting down these

thoughts was that we've found that the feeling of accomplishment, the success and rewards that come from checking IT off one's list, experienced in isolation, is rarely as meaningful and enjoyable as when it's shared with someone else. In our work with corporations, we see so many organizations struggling because their people don't really care about the ebb and flow of each crisis du jour, which are often never completely resolved, and they're content just to collect a paycheck twice a month. Leaders who won't lead because they know the Important Thing for their department would require too much risk, unwelcome collaboration, unrewarded commitment, and overall uncertainty—they simply want to enjoy the serenity of their corner office. Parents who say they value close relationships with their children, but then they allow themselves to drift away into isolation because developing those relationships is hard work. And people who never know the joy and excitement of a life focused on IT, but who succumb to fear that manifests as anger, depression, loneliness, or mere idleness.

With these purposes in mind, we turn to you, dear reader, with two requests.

First, if you were serious about wanting to accomplish the Important Thing in your work or life when you took up this book, don't put it away now that you've reached its end. Use this book as a constant reference. When you're struggling to define IT, or starting IT, or need to communicate IT, or need a reminder to get back to IT, revisit these pages.

Second, share IT. You're not the only one who could benefit from the concepts we've outlined here. Ask yourself, What would our society be like if people agreed on IT, worked together on IT, and had confidence there were solutions, somewhere, while struggling with IT? How would our communities be transformed if we could define IT, help others believe IT, and then work to accomplish IT together? What if every individual you came in contact with was willing to work on IT and ask for help with IT instead of wasting time with unimportant things? Imagine all the times we would get to celebrate achieving IT. Your journey, and that of others, would be different indeed.

Be the one in the meeting who helps the group find clarity on IT. Don't hesitate to seek assistance when you lose your own path toward IT. Set an example for others by the way you strive to achieve IT. Too many of us (present company included) have been settling for something else rather than the Important Thing for far too long.

What's the Song Within You?

Henry David Thoreau offered a powerful and somewhat painful observation: "Most men lead lives of quiet desperation." When you started reading this book, you

*What if every individual
you came in contact with
was willing to work on IT
and ask for help with IT
instead of wasting time
with unimportant things?*

might have identified with that description more readily than you care to admit. *Desperation*, a subtle word, means employing extreme measures in an attempt to escape defeat or frustration—but most of us know the feeling without being given an example.

Your sense of defeat or frustration may come from your awareness of a task at work that never got accomplished. You might have felt it during a difficult time in a relationship or when you gave up on a private goal or dream. Whatever it was, it probably came down to losing sight of the Important Thing.

It's our sincere hope that within these pages we've given you a concrete alternative to desperation, defeat, and frustration. We hope we've set your feet on the right path, but we have no doubt your journey toward IT will not be short, straight, or smooth.

We didn't give you Thoreau's statement in its entirety above. The rest of his thought is so often omitted that many people have never heard it: "Most men lead lives of quiet desperation . . . and go to the grave with the song still in them." Thoreau intended to remind us that we all have some potential, some ability, or some purpose within us that we may never achieve if we don't set aside desperation and take committed, purposeful action.

You now have the tools to deal with unlimited possibilities and limited time. You know the value of planning and completing the Important Thing rather than just processing a bunch of Something Elses from your in-box to your out-box. You know the tools you need to use to determine the possibilities that become an IT in your schedule and then communicate IT to others so they become a support system instead of a drain or distraction.

What's the song within you waiting to be sung? Your Important Thing is waiting. Get to IT.

What's the song within you
waiting to be sung?

Notes

Chapter 3: Believing It

1. Sally Jenkins, "Only Medal for Bode Is Fool's Gold," *Washington Post*, February 26, 2006.
2. Jim Caple, "Miller Solidifies Legacy with Gold," espn.com, February 23, 2010.
3. Ibid.
4. Cam Cole, "Joannie Rochete Faced the Music Alone," *Vancouver Sun*, February 24, 2010.
5. Dina Spector, "Mark Zuckerberg," businessinsider.com, November 22, 2010.
6. Jim Kremer, "J. K. Rowling," collegedropoutshalloffame.com, 2012.
7. about.franchises.com.

Chapter 6: Doing It

1. Adam Gorlick, "Media Multitaskers Pay Mental Price," *Stanford News*, August 24, 2009.
2. Peter Bregman, "How (and Why) to Stop Multitasking," HBR Blog Network, blogs.hbr.org/bregman/2010/05/how-and-why-to-stop-multitaski.html, May 20, 2010.
3. Kerstin Aumann and Ellen Galinsky, "The State of Health in the American Workplace," Families and Work Institute, 2008.

4. Bronwyn Fryer, "Sleep Deficit: The Performance Killer," *Harvard Business Review*, October 2006.
5. Miles Hoffman and Renee Montagne, "Stravinsky's Riotous 'Rite of Spring,'" npr.org, March 21, 2008.

Chapter 7: After Accomplishing It

1. Rachael Rettner, "Study: Happiness Is Experiences, Not Stuff," livescience.com, March 2010.

Chapter 8: Doing It Again

1. New Zealand Air Line Pilots Association, "The Erebus Story: The Loss of TE901," www.erebus.co.nz, 2009.

About the Authors

JONES LOFLIN is an internationally recognized speaker, author, and trainer, and the coauthor of the award-winning book *Juggling Elephants*. For more than nineteen years he has developed and delivered solutions for many Fortune 500 companies in the areas of time management, focus, motivation, change, and work-life balance. Jones has also worked as the trainer of trainers for Who Moved My Cheese? LLC. He lives in North Carolina.

TODD MUSIG is a senior training industry executive, consultant, and author with extensive experience in marketing and business operations. He has been associated with Franklin-Covey, AchieveGlobal, and Who Moved My Cheese? LLC, among other companies. He has worked with such authors as Hyrum Smith, Stephen Covey, and Dr. Spencer Johnson, and he is the coauthor of the award-winning book *Juggling Elephants*. He lives in Utah.

HELP OTHERS
GET TO IT!

To learn more about products and services for individuals and organizations based on *Getting to It,* visit:

www.gettingtoit.com

or call:

1-800-853-4676
336-859-9862
(international)

At gettingtoit.com you can:

- Learn more about keynotes, training programs, and webinars for your organization

- Access FREE resources to further apply the book's principles to your situation

- Connect with the authors

- Subscribe to the Getting to It newsletter and have monthly ideas and resources delivered to your inbox